RAWLS'S *A THEORY OF JUSTICE*

Continuum *Reader's Guides*

Continuum's *Reader's Guides* are clear, concise, and accessible introductions to classic works of philosophy. Each book explores the major themes, historical and philosophical context, and key passages of a major philosophical text, guiding the reader toward a thorough understanding of often demanding material. Ideal for undergraduate students, the guides provide an essential resource for anyone who needs to get to grips with a philosophical text.

Reader's Guides available from Continuum:

Aristotle's Nicomachean Ethics – Christopher Warne
Aristotle's Politics – Judith A. Swanson and C. David Corbin
Berkeley's Principles of Human Knowledge – Alasdair Richmond
Berkeley's Three Dialogues – Aaron Garrett
Deleuze and Guattari's Capitalism and Schizophrenia – Ian Buchanan
Deleuze's Difference and Repetition – Joe Hughes
Derrida's Writing and Difference – Sarah Wood
Descartes' Meditations – Richard Francks
Hegel's Philosophy of Right – David Rose
Heidegger's Being and Time – William Blattner
Heidegger's Later Writings – Lee Braver
Hobbes's Leviathan – Laurie M. Johnson Bagby
Hume's Dialogues Concerning Natural Religion – Andrew Pyle
Hume's Enquiry Concerning Human Understanding – Alan Bailey and Dan O'Brien
Kant's Critique of Aesthetic Judgement – Fiona Hughes
Kant's Critique of Pure Reason – James Luchte
Kant's Groundwork for the Metaphysics of Morals – Paul Guyer
Kierkegaard's Fear and Trembling – Clare Carlisle
Kuhn's The Structure of Scientific Revolutions – John Preston
Locke's Essay Concerning Human Understanding – William Uzgalis
Locke's Second Treatise of Government – Paul Kelly
Mill's On Liberty – Geoffrey Scarre
Mill's Utilitarianism – Henry West
Nietzsche's On the Genealogy of Morals – Daniel Conway
Nietzsche's The Birth of Tragedy – Douglas Burnham and Martin Jesinghausen
Plato's Republic – Luke Purshouse
Plato's Symposium – Thomas L. Cooksey
Rousseau's The Social Contract – Christopher Wraight
Sartre's Being and Nothingness – Sebastian Gardner
Spinoza's Ethics – Thomas J. Cook
Wittgenstein's Tractatus Logico Philosophicus – Roger M. White

RAWLS'S *A THEORY OF JUSTICE*

A Reader's Guide

FRANK LOVETT

continuum

Continuum International Publishing Group
The Tower Building   80 Maiden Lane
11 York Road   Suite 704
London SE1 7NX   New York, NY 10038

www.continuumbooks.com

British Library Cataloguing-in-Publication Data
A catalogue record for this book is available from the British Library.

ISBN: 978-0-8264-3781-5

Library of Congress Cataloging-in-Publication Data
Lovett, Frank.
Rawls's A theory of justice : a reader's guide / Frank Lovett.
p. cm.
Includes bibliographical references.
ISBN: 978-0-8264-3781-5
1. Rawls, John, 1921–2002. Theory of justice. 2. Justice. I. Title.
JC578.R383L58 2010
320.01'1–dc22

2010013372

Typeset by Newgen Imaging Systems Pvt Ltd, Chennai, India

For Liz

CONTENTS

Acknowledgments   viii

1 Introduction and Context   1
  1.1 Biography and historical background   1
  1.2 The philosophical background   4
  1.3 Overview of Rawls's writings   12

2 Overview of Themes   14
  2.1 The main idea of *A Theory of Justice*   14
  2.2 The text: a quick guide   20

3 Reading the Text   23
  3.1 An outline of justice as fairness (§§ 1–3)   23
  3.2 Utilitarianism and intuitionism (§§ 5–8)   30
  3.3 Reflective equilibrium and method (§§ 4, 9)   37
  3.4 The two principles of justice (§§ 10–14)   44
  3.5 Characterizing justice as fairness (§§ 15–17)   65
  3.6 The original position (§§ 20, 22, 24–25)   75
  3.7 The presentation of alternatives (§§ 21, 23)   87
  3.8 The argument for justice as fairness (§§ 26–30, 33)   94
  3.9 The institutions of a just society
      (§§ 31–32, 34–39, 41–43)   110
  3.10 Completing the argument (§§ 40, 44–50)   117
  3.11 Justice and the individual (§§ 18–19, 51–59)   128
  3.12 The search for stability (§§ 60–87)   136

4 Reception and Influence   143
  4.1 *A Theory of Justice* as a classic   143
  4.2 The liberal-communitarian debate   144
  4.3 Further debates and current standing   150

Notes   155
Bibliography and Further Reading   159
Index   163

ACKNOWLEDGMENTS

When I was first invited to write this reader's guide by Sarah Campbell, I naively assumed that it would be a simple matter of transcribing my well-worn lecture notes on Rawls's *A Theory of Justice* into prose. In the event, it not only proved much more challenging, but also much more rewarding than I had anticipated. I would like to thank Ian MacMullen, Ron Watson, and my wife Liz Vickerman for carefully reading and commenting on earlier drafts; Amanda Sabele for helping secure the necessary permissions; Sarah Campbell, Tom Crick, and P. Muralidharan at Continuum Books for guiding the book to print; and finally, my students at Washington University in St. Louis, who have consistently challenged me to understand Rawls better than I might ever have done on my own.

CHAPTER 1

INTRODUCTION AND CONTEXT

1.1 BIOGRAPHY AND HISTORICAL BACKGROUND

John Rawls (1921–2002) was an American political philosopher. His father, William Lee Rawls, was a successful and respected lawyer whose family had moved to Baltimore from the south when he was a child; his mother, Anna Abell Rawls, descended from the formerly affluent Stump family. Both his parents were strongly interested in politics, and his mother in particular campaigned for women's rights with the League of Women Voters. Rawls had four brothers, one older and three younger, two of whom died from illness when he was still young. He attended Princeton University as an undergraduate, completing his AB in philosophy in the fall of 1943. Though he briefly contemplated going on to seminary school to study religion after college, like most of his classmates at that time he chose first to enlist in the army. He served with an intelligence and reconnaissance unit in the Pacific theater for 2 years, earning a Bronze Star, but his experiences there weakened his religious convictions. When he began his graduate studies after the war—again at Princeton—it was in philosophy not religion. Rawls completed his PhD in 1950, writing a dissertation on moral philosophy. During this time he also married Margaret Warfield Fox, with whom he eventually had four children (two daughters and two sons).

After lecturing and extending his studies for two extra years at Princeton, Rawls won a Fulbright scholarship to study at Oxford in the 1952–1953 academic year. There he encountered H. L. A. Hart, Isaiah Berlin, Stuart Hampshire, R. M. Hare, and some other major philosophers of the time, who greatly influenced the development of his own views. On returning to the United States, he landed his first faculty position at Cornell University, where he taught from 1953 until 1959.

He was then a visiting professor at Harvard University (1959–1960), a professor at the Massachusetts Institute of Technology (1960–1962), and finally a permanent member of the philosophy department faculty at Harvard from 1962 until his retirement in 1991. Rawls died at home in 2002.[1]

Rawls's career spanned a particularly eventful period, both in the intellectual history of political and moral philosophy, and in the political and social history of the United States. The philosophical context of Rawls's work will be discussed in more detail in the following section, but it is worth briefly observing here that his field of interest—political and moral philosophy—had for some time been regarded as a field in decline, eclipsed (so it was believed) by other more productive areas of philosophical research. It was only in the 1950s that this trend reversed, and indeed Rawls himself is often retrospectively credited with single-handedly reviving the subject of political philosophy specifically as a respectable and productive field of study. Though this may be something of a simplification, it is nevertheless difficult to overstate his profound influence on later generations of political philosophers and theorists. Even when his views do not command unanimous support (which is often), it is usually the case that the terms of debate and the language employed are ultimately derived from his ideas. It is thus no exaggeration to say that the discipline of political philosophy today owes much of its present form and character to John Rawls.

Before discussing the philosophical context of Rawls's work in more detail, however, it is also worth noting its social and political context. The core ideas that later became the foundation of *A Theory of Justice* were developed during his time at Cornell University in the 1950s. This was a period in which many people, especially after the negative experience of McCarthyism in the early years of the decade, found their commitment to the importance of individual rights renewed, and for some this commitment was further strengthened by their sympathy with the growing civil rights movement in the American South. At the same time, this was a period in which many welfare-state institutions, first introduced during the New Deal, were consolidated and became fully accepted as a permanent feature of American society. The curious thing was that no one had ever really developed a serious philosophical account of how these two commitments—to individual rights and to the welfare state—might be seen as derived from a single, coherent political doctrine. On the contrary, they were often viewed as lying somewhat in tension, with the principles of traditional liberalism supporting the former, and other more leftist doctrines (social democracy, socialism, etc.) supporting the latter.

In this context, it is a striking fact that Rawls's great book does indeed seem to supply just such an account: that is, he derives both a strong commitment to individual rights and also a robust argument for socioeconomic justice from a single, coherent philosophical theory. It is no surprise then that Rawls's contribution has often been described in this way—as having supplied a philosophical rationale for the modern liberal's support for both individual rights and the welfare state. But it would be a mistake to reduce our account of Rawls to this simplistic story. For one thing, he did not actually support the welfare-state institutions in the particular form they assumed in the United States. For another, his motivations were actually much more complex, and connected to deeper philosophical problems of longer standing importance than the mere providing of intellectual support to the American Democratic Party's platform. Crude reductions of a sophisticated philosophical work to the historical conditions in which it was written often cost more insight than they gain.

Rawls did not support welfare state.

The core ideas underlying *A Theory of Justice* were largely formulated, as I have said, in the 1950s. Rawls actually wrote his book, however, during the 1960s, and it did not finally appear in print until 1971. These were, of course, particularly turbulent times in American history: the struggle for desegregation, the Vietnam War, the student protests, and so on, clearly left their own imprint on Rawls's thinking. Although neither these, nor indeed any other contemporary political or social events, are ever explicitly discussed in *A Theory of Justice*—which maintains throughout a singularly detached and philosophical point of view—their traces are nevertheless unmistakable in the final form of that work, as we shall see in due course. In the remainder of this introduction, however, we will concentrate on the intellectual, rather than the social, context.

1.2 THE PHILOSOPHICAL BACKGROUND

1.2.1 Utilitarianism and intuitionism

As we have seen, Rawls started writing *A Theory of Justice* near the end of the 1950s, and continued to develop his work throughout the 1960s. At this time, the dominant tradition in moral and political philosophy was utilitarianism, and it had held this position of dominance for nearly a century. Not surprisingly, Rawls discusses utilitarianism extensively in his work, and so shall we. For now, it will be enough to state the main idea of the theory, which is extremely simple and, at least initially, eminently plausible. Basically, utilitarianism holds that actions, laws, institutions, and so on can be judged as better or worse according to their tendency to maximize the sum total happiness of individual persons, counting the happiness of each person equally.

When introduced by the English philosopher Jeremy Bentham (1748–1832) in the late eighteenth century, utilitarianism was a striking—even radical—philosophical doctrine. For one thing, it swept away any and all references to God's will, to the interests of society, to customs and traditions, to the natural law, and so on. In place of these, it advanced what was thought to be the straightforwardly rational and scientific procedure of simply measuring the happiness of each individual person, and then adding up this happiness across the whole of a population. In this respect, utilitarianism was obviously a product of the Enlightenment Age—a time of great faith in the promise of reason and the scientific method on the one hand, and of distrust in religion, superstition, and tradition on the other. Another remarkable, and indeed potentially revolutionary, feature of utilitarianism was its insistence on counting the happiness of all persons exactly the same: the happiness of kings and nobles count no more or less than the happiness of tradesmen and peasants, the happiness of Englishmen no more than the happiness of Frenchmen, and so on. In this vein, Bentham's most important and influential disciple, John Stuart Mill (1806–1873), later went on to argue that since the happiness of men should count no more than the happiness of women, the many existing social and legal inequalities between the sexes ought to be eliminated. For many people in the eighteenth and nineteenth centuries, these were difficult claims to swallow.

In time, of course, utilitarianism was bound to seem less radical as people became more used to the idea of the equal moral worth of all human beings. Thus, the features of utilitarianism that we have so far mentioned cannot fully account for its continued dominance well into the twentieth century. This persistence can better be explained by some of its other somewhat more subtle and conceptual virtues. The most important of these are utilitarianism's completeness and decisiveness: there is no possible moral, political, or social question to which utilitarianism cannot, at least in principle, provide a definite and consistent answer. This makes it an extremely powerful theory. It also sets the bar very high for potential competitors, as can be illustrated by the failure of another theory, popular in some philosophical circles during the first half of the twentieth century, called intuitionism.

To appreciate the motivations behind intuitionism, we must first understand that while utilitarianism was far and away the dominant theory, by no means was everyone completely happy with it. Let me explain. Suppose that Andrea promises to give $100 to Bob, perhaps to repay some favor he has done for her, but that she later finds it would be extremely inconvenient for her to do so. Our common sense moral intuition strongly suggests that Andrea nevertheless lies under some sort of obligation to do what she promised, despite the inconvenience. The difficulty is that utilitarianism apparently tells us our intuitions here might be wrong. If, for example, the unhappiness Andrea would experience in keeping her promise would be significantly greater than the unhappiness Bob would experience if she reneged, then it seems utilitarianism recommends the latter course of action. Many people were not satisfied with this conclusion. To give another example, suppose that Andrea commits a violent crime. Again, our common sense moral intuition suggests that she— and she alone—deserves to be punished. Utilitarianism, however, does not necessarily support this intuition. Since any punishment would presumably reduce Andrea's happiness, we must show that the punishment serves some useful purpose to counterbalance this loss. This further purpose might be deterrence,

Utilitarian principle of max happiness sometimes contradicts with human intuitions.

for example: if Andrea is punished, then fewer people will commit violent crimes in the future, and the overall happiness will be increased. But notice that, on the utilitarian view, there is no sense in which Andrea specifically deserves her punishment. Indeed, if we have trouble apprehending Andrea, we might accomplish an equivalent deterrence by framing the innocent Bob and punishing him instead. Practical difficulties aside, utilitarianism does not give us a reason to regard such tactics as morally unacceptable from the start.

Thus we see that, despite its initial plausibility, when carefully thought out utilitarianism can diverge significantly from common sense morality. This fact was recognized on all sides; the debate was only what to do about it. Some proposed an alternative theory. Perhaps our common sense morality is broadly correct, they argued. Perhaps our stronger intuitions in such cases are revealing to us the basic structure of morality, which consists in a set of primitive moral principles such as fidelity, desert, beneficence, and so on. Glossing over some complicated details of less importance to our story, this is roughly the view called "intuitionism." Intuitionism provided an alternative for those who were deeply unsatisfied with utilitarianism, and this explains why some were attracted to it in the early part of the twentieth century.

But it is also easy to see why intuitionism could never have supplanted utilitarianism as the dominant theory. Intuitionism does little more than give us a name for what remains only a heap of intuitions. What are we supposed to do, for example, when our obligation to keep a promise conflicts with our obligation not to harm others? Intuitions alone give us no clear guidance. In other words, the theory is woefully incomplete, and here the great strength of utilitarianism, which can answer any possible question, comes fully into view. Given this strength, one might just as plausibly conclude that we should doubt our intuitions whenever they diverge from utilitarianism, rather than the other way around. After all, our intuitions might simply be the product of a biased upbringing or inadequate education. Why place such faith in their accuracy? Utilitarianism could only ever have been supplanted by a competing theory with comparable conceptual power, and so it long remained dominant despite the lingering uneasiness among some moral and political philosophers.

This was more or less the situation when Rawls began his work, as he clearly indicates in his preface to *A Theory of Justice.* "During much of modern moral philosophy the predominant systematic theory has been some form of utilitarianism," he writes. Those who criticized utilitarianism "noted the apparent incongruities between many of its implications and our moral sentiments. But they failed . . . to construct a workable and systematic moral conception to oppose it." Rawls aimed to rectify this situation—that is, to "offer an alternative systematic account of justice that is superior . . . to the dominant utilitarianism of the tradition" (vii–viii; xvii–xviii Rev.).[2] The alternative he offers is called "justice as fairness," and the basic point of his book is simply to explain and defend this alternative, as against utilitarianism in particular.

1.2.2 The social contract tradition

By no means did Rawls invent his theory of justice as fairness from whole cloth. Indeed, though this considerably understates his achievement, he denied that his theory was especially original. Again quoting from the preface, he says that he merely attempted "to generalize and carry to a higher order of abstraction the traditional theory of the social contract as represented by Locke, Rousseau, and Kant" (viii; xviii Rev.). Since Rawls himself draws our attention to these authors, we should perhaps briefly review their ideas as further background to our reading. Interestingly, each of these authors predates the introduction of utilitarianism. This may lead us to wonder first, why their views were supplanted by utilitarianism in the nineteenth century, and second, what Rawls saw in their writings that others had missed.

The traditional theory of the social contract, to which Rawls refers, was popular in the seventeenth and eighteenth centuries, reaching its peak historical influence around the time of the American and (at least initially) French Revolutions. It was itself a combination and reworking of two even older ideas, both of which can be traced back to the medieval period, if not earlier. The first was the idea of what was called a "state of nature"—an imagined time in human history before the introduction of political authority and social institutions. This notion of a state of nature was thought helpful in distinguishing between what

7

was natural and what artificial in human affairs. For example, we might wonder whether there would be something like private property in a state of nature, in which case we should regard this as a "natural"—not merely a politically or socially constructed—phenomenon. The second was the idea that government rested in some sense on a sort of original agreement or compact between rulers and subjects. This original compact might be expressed in a coronation oath, for example, according to which the king agrees to rule justly and benevolently, while the people in turn pledge obedience to his commands.

Both ideas had been around for a long time when, in the seventeenth century, it occurred to some writers that they might be combined into a single theory. Roughly speaking, we start by imagining people living in a state of nature, without a government. We then reflect on the various disadvantages of this condition, as for example the fact that people's lives and possessions are not very secure in such a state. It stands to reason that such people would soon gather together with the intention of ending the state of nature and setting up some sort of government. The upshot of this process would be a social contract—that is, an agreement setting out the terms according to which a government would be formed, and the conditions under which it would subsequently operate. Since people in the state of nature would aim to overcome certain specific problems only, it was usually held that the authority of any government they created would thus be limited to those particular areas of competence—no sensible person, it was thought, would voluntarily give up more of their natural liberty than was absolutely necessary. The canonical statement of this doctrine was set out in the writings of John Locke (1632–1704), which exercised great influence on people like Thomas Jefferson: when Jefferson wrote in the Declaration of Independence that governments are instituted to secure unalienable rights, that they derive their just powers from the consent of the governed, and so forth, it was obvious to his contemporaries that he was reciting the familiar doctrine of the social contract.

Despite its influence, within a generation or two the social contract theory had more or less been thoroughly discredited. Why was this? One reason was that, with improved historiography, it became increasingly obvious that the idea of a state

[handwritten margin note: People's lives & property are not secure in a state of nature]

of nature was pure fiction. What can a manifestly false story tell us about how we ought to organize societies here and now? Another reason was that it could fairly easily be shown that hardly anyone actually does consent to their particular government. For the most part, we are born wherever we are born, and (to varying degrees) we simply put up with the government we have. Now there is a lot more to be said here, and the traditional theory of the social contract in fact had coherent answers to these objections, which for the purposes of understanding Rawls's theory we need not go into. The relevant point is simply that these objections were generally regarded as decisive, and so the theory fell by the wayside once utilitarianism came along.

1.2.3 The moral philosophy of Kant

Of the other two figures explicitly mentioned by Rawls— Jean-Jacques Rousseau (1712–1778) and Immanuel Kant (1724–1804)—Kant is the more important for our particular story. Though certainly interesting and important in his own right, we may here simply note that Rousseau served as a sort of transitional figure between Locke and Kant. It is arguably Kant, more than any single other philosopher, who provided the inspiration for Rawls's own work. Unfortunately, Kant's immensely influential writings, which cover a vast range of philosophical topics, are notoriously difficult to read and understand. Here we will discuss only one aspect of his writings on moral philosophy especially significant in appreciating Rawls's views.

In 1785, Kant published a short but dense book with an imposing title—the *Groundwork of the Metaphysics of Morals*. To simplify somewhat, this essay poses and attempts to solve a very abstract and general philosophical problem. In most of our various actions which are not simply reflex responses or unthinking habits, we tend to act on the basis of whatever reasons seem good to us. For example, despite her desire to sleep in some days, we might imagine that Andrea dutifully rises promptly every morning because she believes she has a good reason to arrive on time for her classes in business school. Now most of us, most of the time, want our reasons not only to *seem* good, but to actually *be* good—that is, we want to be acting on the basis of what might be termed *valid* reasons. (If it turned out that she did not really have to be on time for class, Andrea would understandably be annoyed, and would probably change her behavior accordingly.) It is thus an interesting philosophical question what, if anything, can actually make our reasons valid or invalid.

To answer this question, Kant divides the sorts of reasons we might have into two groups. In the first group are what we might describe as instrumental reasons. Suppose that Andrea wants to be rich, and further suppose that attending business school will increase the probability that she will indeed become rich. It seems to follow, then, that she does indeed have a reason—a valid reason—for attending business school. The validity of instrumental reasons is supplied by our goals or aims, together with some facts about the world. Somewhat confusingly, Kant terms the commands issuing from valid instrumental reasons like this "hypothetical imperatives" (hypothetical only in the sense that their validity depends on the existence of the relevant goal or aim, which might or might not be present in a given case or for a given person). These are contrasted with another group of reasons, which are not instrumental. Consider whether we have a good reason to rescue a baby that falls into a nearby pool when no one else is around to help. If we do have such a reason, it would not seem to be contingent on our particular goals or aims. Some people, for example, want to be praised as morally virtuous, whereas others are indifferent to such praise; both sorts of people, however, *ought* to rescue the baby (though, admittedly, the second might be less *likely* to do so). Kant terms the commands issuing from valid noninstrumental reasons like this "categorical imperatives."

As we have seen, it is relatively easy to explain why hypothetical imperatives are valid. The real difficulty—and Kant's special contribution—lies in explaining why categorical imperatives are valid. He argues that there is a unique decision rule for determining whether something is a categorical imperative or not. To make things even more confusing, however, he also offers several formulations—five, by most counts—of this unique decision rule, which are supposed to be equivalent. Only two will be mentioned here. The first is called the formula of humanity, which instructs you to act such that "you use humanity, whether in your own person or in the person of any other, always at the same time as an end, never merely as a means" (Kant 1785: 38). In other words, we should not treat people as if they were simply instruments for our own particular purposes. The other, even more famous formulation is called the formula of universal law, which instructs you to "act only in accordance with that maxim through which you can at the same time will that it become a universal law" (ibid.: 31). What is interesting about this proposal is that, although this was not widely recognized at first, it can address some of the problems (discussed above) that bedeviled utilitarianism. Consider Andrea's decision as to whether to keep her promise to pay Bob $100. This decision can be described as a choice between two competing maxims: according to the first, people should keep their promises if they are able to do so; according to the second, people should keep their promises only if it is convenient for them to do so. Which maxim would Andrea want to be the universal law—that is, the rule for everyone, including herself, to follow? If she were sensible, clearly the first and not the second. This, according to Kant, tells us that the first is a valid categorical imperative.

Despite the promise of this line of reasoning, Kant's moral philosophy was for some time not developed into a theory able to compete with utilitarianism. Partly, this was due to the fact that the opaqueness of his writing prevented many people from fully understanding his ideas; indeed, for some time it was thought that Kant's moral philosophy, if intelligible at all, was effectively equivalent to utilitarianism! However, this was not the only problem. Another was that the formula of universal law, at least as presented in Kant's work, had some serious loopholes. To see this, we must first observe that although the maxim of our action should be universal in the sense that everyone should follow the same maxim, there is nothing in the theory requiring that the maxim treat everyone the same. Nor should there be: the maxim, "provide disabled persons (but not others) wheelchairs" is a perfectly sensible maxim that we might want everyone to follow. But if this maxim is permissible, what's wrong with the maxim, "always discriminate against minorities (but not others)?" If Andrea is not herself a minority, it is perfectly con-sistent for her to want everyone, including herself, to follow this maxim, and that seems sufficient, on the formula of universal law, to demonstrate that her discriminatory behavior is supported by valid reasons. This does not seem right.

Today, there are of course many sophisticated treatments of Kantian moral philosophy that help us surmount difficulties like these. But all this came later. When Rawls began his work in the 1950s, Kant was still a relatively obscure figure in the history of philosophy, the social contract tradition was regarded as effectively dead, and utilitarianism was the only real game in town. Rawls's genius was to realize what apparently no one else had realized before: namely, that the ideas found in the writings of past figures such as Locke and Kant, for all their flaws, could be reworked with greater sophistication into a powerful theory that presented a real challenge to utilitarianism. Beginning in the next chapter, we will see how Rawls tries to do this.

1.3 OVERVIEW OF RAWLS'S WRITINGS

The focus of this Reader's Guide will be Rawls's most important work, *A Theory of Justice*. This book, as we have seen, was largely written in the 1960s and finally appeared in print in 1971. A few years later, a German translation was commissioned, and in the process of supplying the manuscript for this translation, Rawls introduced a number of textual revisions. Although these changes were made around 1975, the revised version of the text was not published in English until 1999. Most of these changes are minor, and the two editions will usually be treated here as interchangeable apart from their differing pagination; the few differences in substance will be mentioned when they arise.

Rawls wrote much else besides *A Theory of Justice*, however, and thus it might be helpful to place this work in context relative to some of his other writings. In the years before the publication of *A Theory of Justice*, Rawls initially proposed many of its main arguments in a series of essays that appeared in specialized philosophy journals. Three of these are particularly worthy of note. In "Outline of a Decision Procedure for Ethics" (1951), he develops a foundational account of justification in moral and political philosophy. The basic idea—what he refers to as "reflective equilibrium"—underlies all of his writings on moral and political philosophy, and indeed it has influenced many philosophers quite independently of the line of argument stemming from *A Theory of Justice*. In "Two Concepts of Rules" (1955), Rawls frames utilitarianism—the theory he ultimately sets out to defeat—in a compelling manner, as a theory addressed to the particular sorts of problems in political philosophy he is most interested in. (Roughly speaking, as we shall see in the next chapter, he presents it as an attractive theory of social justice.) One reason for doing this, perhaps, is that the more sympathetic his presentation of utilitarianism, the more convincing his answer to it will ultimately be. Finally, in "Justice as Fairness" (1958), he lays out the core of his argument for an alternative to utilitarianism. This paper represented a sort of trial run for the book.

Some time after publishing *A Theory of Justice* in 1971, Rawls began to fundamentally reconsider some important aspects of his theory. The details of this shift are extremely complex and largely beyond the scope of this Reader's Guide, though it is important to be aware that the shift happened. Rawls's reconsiderations initially appeared, again, in a series of papers, the three most important of which were "Kantian Constructivism in Moral Theory" (1980), "Social Unity and Primary Goods" (1982), and "Justice as Fairness: Political Not Metaphysical" (1985). Eventually, as Rawls finally worked out all the inter-related dimensions of his new views, he published a second major book, *Political Liberalism* in 1993. This is an extremely difficult book, in many ways unintelligible to the reader not already familiar to some extent with the ideas in *A Theory of Justice*. These two works together, which combined run to nearly a thousand pages, stand as his received view on most issues.

This is a Reader's Guide to *A Theory of Justice* only. References will generally be made to the later changes in Rawls's views only insofar as they aid in our better understanding of that text. For those interested in Rawls's final views, but intimidated by the prospect of reading both his massive treatises, there exists also a much shorter presentation under the title, *Justice as Fairness: A Restatement* (2001). This is not exactly a book written by Rawls, but rather a series of lectures he delivered at Harvard, which usefully summarize and collate the arguments from his two main books. Though not a substitute for *A Theory of Justice* and *Political Liberalism*, these lectures do provide an extremely valuable overall introduction to his final views, and can serve as a handy rough-and-ready guide as to how everything is supposed to fit together.

CHAPTER 2

OVERVIEW OF THEMES

2.1 THE MAIN IDEA OF *A THEORY OF JUSTICE*

A Theory of Justice is a long and dense work, running nearly 600 pages, and it is easy to get lost in the details. Accordingly, it is helpful to approach the text with an overall sense of what Rawls is trying to argue. The present chapter aims to provide this, together with a rough guide for navigating the lengthy text. Fortunately, the main idea of Rawls's argument is relatively easy to appreciate.

Recall from Chapter 1 that when Rawls first developed his views, two theories of moral and political philosophy were in the field. The first and dominant theory, of course, was utilitarianism. To most minds, nothing else seemed remotely as powerful or sophisticated. But at the same time, many people admitted that utilitarianism had a number of troubling features, some of which were previously discussed. Here we may consider yet another. Imagine some society in which a small minority of the population is held in abject slavery. These slaves are quite unhappy, of course, but everyone else is somewhat happier than they would otherwise be since the slaves are made to perform many of the more onerous jobs in that society. Now it might turn out that when we add up the improvements to the happiness of the majority we get a much larger sum than the total of the unhappiness inflicted on the slaves, even though each individual slave is very unhappy indeed. In this society, utilitarianism would seem to endorse the institution of slavery. Now of course we would hope that the numbers will not turn out this way, and indeed they probably would not. But should this matter? Put another way, should the justice or injustice of slavery hinge on what the numbers happen to show? Many people have the strong moral intuition that the answer is *no*—that it shouldn't matter whether the happiness of the majority outweighs the unhappiness of the slaves, since the enslavement of human beings is simply wrong on its face.

The difficulty, of course, is that this is no more than an intuition. Which brings us to the other theory of moral and political philosophy—namely, intuitionism. But as we discussed in the previous chapter, intuitionism turns out not to really be a theory at all, so much as a name given to an unsystematic jumble of moral intuitions we happen to have. Intuitionism could not hope to defeat utilitarianism because it had no answer to what we should do in the many cases where our intuitions are incomplete, vague, or (worst of all) in conflict with one another. Rawls thought we needed a better theory—a theory as powerful and systematic as utilitarianism, but better able to give an account of our moral intuitions, as for example that the institution of slavery is intrinsically wrong. What would such a theory be like?

In order to give an overall sense of how Rawls set out to address this challenge, it is first necessary to introduce some foundational ideas. We will be returning to these ideas in greater detail when we discuss the relevant passages in the text; for now, it is enough to have a general sense of their significance. The first of these is the idea of society as what is called "a system of cooperation." This is a way of thinking about what a society is or, at any rate, what its most important and characteristic features are, and it can be illustrated simply as follows. Imagine three friends who want to start a new company together. One is a good product designer, the second has a talent for marketing, and the third is an experienced accountant. Working together, their partnership will succeed and earn lots of money, but they cannot succeed working independently or in competition with one another. Suppose they do agree to work together. At some point, they will have to decide how to divide the profits of their new firm. What would be a good rule for doing this? The product designer could argue that without a product, there would be nothing to sell; since her contribution is the most fundamental, she should receive the lion's share of the profits. The marketer, in turn, could argue that without his efforts, they would have no customers, and thus no profits; therefore, his share of the profits should be the largest. And so on. What is important to notice here is that it is better for all that they agree on *some* rule, because there would be no partnership otherwise, and thus no profits to divide; but at the same time, they might each have conflicting ideas about *which* rule should be agreed on since different rules would favor different parties. Their partnership is thus mutually beneficial, while at the same time being a source of potential disagreement.

Rawls believes that we can think of a society in much the same way, albeit on a much larger and more complex scale. As he puts it,

> . . . a society is a more or less self-sufficient association of persons who in their relations to one another recognize certain rules of conduct as binding and who for the most part act in accordance with them. Suppose further that these rules specify a system of cooperation designed to advance the good of those taking part in it. Then, although a society is a cooperative venture for mutual advantage, it is typically marked by a conflict as well as by an identity of interests. (4; 4 Rev.)

Consider, for instance, how jobs are filled in different societies. In feudal societies, jobs are often assigned by birth: thus, if your father was a silversmith, you are also a silversmith; if your father was a peasant farmer, you are too; and so on. In societies with command economies, by contrast, jobs are assigned by government planners, who are supposed to allocate jobs according to some assessment of your abilities and the needs of the community. In capitalist societies, jobs are assigned through the mechanism of the labor market, governed not only by the laws of supply and demand, but also by labor regulations, licensing requirements, and so forth. These are examples of the sorts of "rules of conduct" specifying "a system of cooperation" that Rawls has in mind. Since these rules "advance the good of those taking part" (we all benefit from the division of labor, for example), we can regard society as "a cooperative venture for mutual advantage." But at the same time, since one configuration of rules might favor some people and a different configuration others, society is "typically marked by a conflict as well as by an identity of interests." The challenge lies in deciding which system of cooperation would be best for all.

This brings us to the second foundational idea in Rawls's thinking: the idea of what he calls the "basic structure of a society," which he defines as "the way in which the major social institutions distribute fundamental rights and duties and determine the division of advantages from social cooperation" (7; 6 Rev.). We can best get a sense of what he means here with the help of another simple illustration. Consider two members of some society, Andrea and Bob. Let us suppose they are more or less equally intelligent and equally capable individuals, but that Andrea is hardworking whereas Bob is lazy. Now if we asked whose life we would expect on the whole to go better (in a conventional sense), other things being equal, we would probably assume that Andrea's would. But this might not always be the case: much depends on what sort of society they happen to live in. For example, imagine that they lived in a feudal society, and that Andrea was born a peasant and Bob to nobility. Even if Andrea puts forth considerably more effort than Bob, her life will probably go much less well, on nearly any reasonable measure, than Bob's. Or imagine that Andrea was born a slave in the American South of the early nineteenth century, whereas Bob was born the son of a plantation owner: again, Andrea's life will probably go less well, despite her best efforts. What these examples suggest is that how well our lives go is only partly due to our individual efforts. This is not to say, of course, that individual effort counts for nothing—Andrea will probably do better for herself by working hard than otherwise. The point is only that the particular organization of society will often play some considerable role.

This is roughly what Rawls means by the "basic structure" of society: the basic structure is the set of social institutions and practices that systematically influence how well our lives can be expected to go, individual effort aside. These institutions and practices obviously include such things as the system of government and laws, but they also include some less obvious things, such as the organization of the economy and, in some cases, cultural conditions. As an example of the first, suppose that Bob happens to have a natural gift for hitting home runs. How well his life goes will depend partly on the effort he puts into cultivating this talent, but it will also depend partly on the structure of the economy: if there is a free market for baseball talent, his life might go much better than if there is not. As an example of the second, suppose that Andrea is born into a deeply sexist society. Even if this general sexism is not reflected in official laws and policies, it is still the case that her life will probably go less well than it would if she lived in a less sexist society. Thus we see that the idea of the basic structure of society is an extremely broad and abstract one: it includes all those institutions and practices—legal, economic, and cultural—that together constitute the background conditions or social environment within which the individual members of a society live out their lives as best they can, according to their own designs.

Although this idea of a basic structure is extremely broad and abstract, it actually provides Rawls with a basis for narrowing his dispute with utilitarianism. This is because utilitarianism has often been interpreted as not merely a theory about how societies ought to be organized, but indeed as a complete moral philosophy. That is to say, we might regard utilitarianism as not only a providing an answer to whether the institution of slavery is acceptable or not, but also as providing an answer as to whether I ought to lie to a friend in order to protect his feelings, whether I ought to spend my pay-raise on a new car or donate it to charity, and so forth. It is debated whether the broader or the narrower interpretation of utilitarianism is better, and also which the founders of utilitarianism (Bentham, Mill, and the others) really had in mind, but we may leave these debates aside in discussing Rawls. What is important here is that *A Theory of Justice* addresses utilitarianism in the narrower sense, as a theory of what might be called social justice.[1]

That is, if we think of a society as a mutually beneficial system of cooperation (as discussed above), and if we think of the basic structure of that society as setting the main terms of cooperation, then we may think of a theory of social justice as an account of which feasible basic structure would best exemplify the virtue of being just. In Rawls's words, the basic structure is "the subject of justice" (7; 6 Rev.). From this point of view, utilitarianism is the theory according to which the most just basic structure would be the one that would tend to maximize the sum total happiness of a society's members, counting the happiness of each member equally. Without worrying about whether utilitarianism could serve a plausible account of morality in general, we can ask more narrowly whether it is the best account of social justice. In Rawls's view, it is not. So what account does he think would be better?

In order to appreciate his alternative proposal, we can again resort to a simple illustration. Imagine that a wealthy cattle rancher has died and left his heard of cattle to his two sons, without specifying which cows were to go to which son in particular. Now every cow has its own unique characteristics, so dividing the herd is not so simple as counting them off into two numerically equal groups, or giving all the brown cows to one brother and all the black cows to the other. Since the brothers get into a bit of a quarrel over the division, they decide to consult a wise judge. How does he proceed? The answer is simple. The judge turns to one brother and says, "Divide the herd into two lots, however you please"; then turning to the other brother he adds, "Once your brother has divided the herd, you choose which of the two lots will be yours and which will be his." This will strike many people as an eminently fair procedure. Since the first brother can assume that the second will choose the better lot, if there is one, he is compelled to divide the herd as fairly as possible, so that he will be satisfied with whatever lot is left for him. Now Rawls's theory of social justice—what he calls "justice as fairness"—is essentially based on the same idea.[2]   veil of ignorance

On his view, the most just basic structure for a society is the one you would choose if you did not know what your particular role in that society's system of cooperation was going to be. That is to say, you might turn out to be a wealthy captain of industry, or you might turn out to be a work-a-day street cleaner. The question is, what sort of society would you want to live in, if you did not know? Our answer to this question gives us an account of a just society. It is an extremely compelling idea, and the whole point of *A Theory of Justice* is simply to work out in elaborate detail this single, basic thought.

Before plunging into these details, however, it is worth noting how Rawls brings together various ideas discussed in the previous chapter. He first draws from Locke the notion of a social contract, but manages to dispense with the historical baggage once associated with that doctrine: we need not imagine that people ever lived in a state of nature, nor that people ever actually offer their consent to a particular government. For Rawls, the question posed above is merely hypothetical—a thought experiment. Also notice that the content of the social contract has shifted in an important way: rather than being an agreement concerning a form of government, the social contract imagined by Rawls is an agreement concerning the basic structure of society. In place of a state of nature, Rawls imagines that people are asked to choose a basic structure from within what he calls an "original position." Since you are not supposed to know what your particular role in the society is going to be, he says that in the original position you would have to choose from behind "a veil of ignorance." This idea of a veil of ignorance brings in Kant's moral philosophy: it forces you to choose a basic structure using strictly impartial criteria. That is roughly what the formula of universal law was supposed to do, but the veil of ignorance does it better. Would you choose to live in a sexist society? Of course not, since you could not be sure whether you were going to be a man or a woman. Would you choose to live in a society with the institution of slavery? Of course not, since you might turn out to be one of the slaves. This is the basic thought process, though Rawls actually carries it out in a manner that is considerably more abstract. Rather than choosing specific institutions, he imagines that you would choose general principles that would guide the design of specific institutions. His argument is that in an original position behind the veil of ignorance you would not choose utilitarian general principles, you would choose the principles of justice as fairness instead.

2.2 THE TEXT: A QUICK GUIDE

With this overview in mind, let us review the table of contents to *A Theory of Justice*. The text is obviously divided into three parts of three chapters each. These chapters, however, are unusually long—running 50 pages or more in length. If one were to attempt reading the text straight through, it would soon be apparent that the chapters cover many diverse topics not always connected in some obvious way by a single coherent theme. This is no doubt partly due to the manner in which the book was written. Sometime around the mid 1960s, Rawls completed a draft of *A Theory of Justice*, which was much shorter than the final version. For many years this manuscript circulated among students and colleagues who provided Rawls with extensive critical feedback. This was also a time of great social and political upheaval in the United States and elsewhere (as noted in the previous chapter). Reflections on these events, together with the critical feedback of his readers, naturally led Rawls to further develop his ideas. Since he was writing without the benefit of computers, however, introducing changes to the text was no easy matter. Most often, therefore, his revisions took the form of new material that was written out separately. These additional materials were then assigned a letter code (A, B, C, etc.) indicating where they should be inserted into the original text. Obviously, this procedure did not lend itself to the creation of a streamlined final manuscript! The result was a very lengthy book with sprawling chapters.

Fortunately for us, Rawls chose to divide each of his chapters into sections. These 87 consecutively numbered sections are for most people the main reading units of the book. Each runs a more digestible five to ten pages, and each usually addresses a single, more or less coherent theme. One need not, and indeed many people do not, read these numbered sections in strictly consecutive order. For example, a perfectly respectable reading plan that divides the whole text into 5 blocks of 50 or so pages each might look something like this:

- §§ 1–9: these sections introduce the main argument of *A Theory of Justice*, and set up the contrast between justice as fairness and utilitarianism.
- §§ 11–17, 68: these sections describe in detail the two principles of justice that constitute his theory of justice as fairness.
- §§ 20–26, 33, 29, 40: these sections present the original position argument for justice as fairness over utilitarianism.
- §§ 31, 34–37, 43, 47–48: these sections discuss how justice as fairness might be implemented in the design of major social and political institutions.
- §§ 44, 46, 18–19, 55–59, 87: finally, these sections address the difficult problems of intergenerational justice and civil disobedience, together with Rawls's conclusion.

This reading plan only adds up to about half the overall text; also, it is obviously a reading plan heavily weighted towards the first two-thirds of the book. This is no accident. Broadly speaking, the last third of *A Theory of Justice* is devoted to what Rawls called "the problem of stability"—this is, roughly, the problem of showing how people living in a society governed by the principles of justice as fairness would come to embrace and support those principles, rather than reject and resist them. In the previous chapter, however, we noted that sometime after publishing his book in 1971, Rawls began reconsidering many of his views, especially as they related to precisely this problem. Since Rawls himself regarded the views he later presented in *Political Liberalism* (1993) as superceding the argument in part three of *A Theory of Justice*, it is customary to give part three much less attention than the earlier two parts of *A Theory of Justice*, which he more or less remained committed to.

This Reader's Guide, however, is intended to be comprehensive. Accordingly, we will progress through the text more or less in sequential order, offering at least some guidance for all parts of the text, though not always with equal attention. In this way it will be easier for the reader to find his or her way through the text, regardless of their particular interests or reading plan.

CHAPTER 3

READING THE TEXT

3.1 AN OUTLINE OF JUSTICE AS FAIRNESS (§§ 1–3)

In the first three sections of *A Theory of Justice*, Rawls conveniently provides a broad overview of his account of social justice. In the process of doing this, he introduces some of the fundamental ideas that underlie his whole way of thinking about such questions. Our understanding of the text as a whole will thus be greatly served by carefully attending to these opening sections.

In § 1, Rawls puts forward two bold assertions. Social institutions, we might think, can be regarded as better or worse for a whole host of reasons: they might be more or less economically efficient, for example, or they might reflect a community's traditional values to a greater or lesser extent. But Rawls asserts that

> Justice is the first virtue of social institutions, as truth is of systems of thought. A theory however elegant and economical must be rejected or revised if it is untrue; likewise laws and institutions no matter how efficient and well-arranged must be reformed or abolished if they are unjust. (3; 3 Rev.)

In Chapter 2, we discussed the institution of slavery. Suppose it happened that slavery was a very economically efficient way of allocating certain forms of labor in some society. Rawls is saying here that this should not matter: justice is more important than economic efficiency. This is his first assertion. His second is that every "person possesses an inviolability founded on justice that even the welfare of society as a whole cannot override. For this reason justice denies that the loss of freedom for some is made right by a greater good shared by others" (3–4; 3 Rev.). Slavery again provides a helpful illustration here: even if the happiness of society as a whole were enhanced by enslaving a few, it would not be just for us to do so. Or, suppose that society as a whole could be made more secure from terrorism by simply locking up all potential terrorists without trial. This too would not be just. Often we express this thought by saying that people must have at least some fundamental or inalienable rights.

It is important to understand that Rawls does not pretend these two opening assertions constitute arguments. Although they express what many people actually believe, they are as yet no more than intuitions; even if to some extent they are true, they are probably "expressed too strongly," as he puts it (4; 4 Rev.). We should observe, however, that utilitarianism—the dominant theory of social justice when Rawls was writing— would have a difficult time accounting for either intuition. Rawls proposes that we explore whether some other theory might better account for both in a compelling and systematic manner. If successful, we might find that, contrary to what utilitarianism suggests, these intuitions are on the whole sound.

To this end, Rawls proceeds to lay down some conceptual building blocks for a competing theory. He begins with the idea of society as a system of cooperation, which we discussed earlier in Chapter 2. This is the thought that one can conceive of a society as a complex system for coordinating the activities of many different people for their mutual benefit. Now in any society, there are many ways this coordination might feasibly be organized. Since different systems of cooperation will benefit different members of society to a greater or lesser extent, some sort of principle or set of principles are needed to help us choose among the alternatives. Among these, says Rawls, "are the principles of social justice: they provide a way of assigning rights and duties in the basic institutions of society and they define the appropriate distribution of benefits and burdens of social cooperation" (4; 4 Rev.). For example, we might compare the current configuration of institutions in the United States with a possible alternative the same in most respects except that it includes some sort of national health care system. Each of these configurations would assign responsibilities and distribute benefits and burdens somewhat differently. Which is to be preferred? Principles of social justice supply one answer to this question.

This brings us to Rawls's second building block, which we also discussed in Chapter 2: the idea of the basic structure of society. The basic structure, recall, is the configuration of institutions and practices—legal, economic, and cultural—that together constitute the background conditions against which the individual members of a society live out their lives according to their own designs. While the basic structure does not fully determine how well any given person's life will go—individual effort, luck, and other factors will undoubtedly also play a role—it is especially significant that whatever effects the basic structure does have, they will be effects for which the individual herself cannot plausibly be held responsible. In this sprit, Rawls remarks that,

All institutions have inequalities that put then @ different starting Points.

> ... the institutions of society favor certain starting positions over others. These are especially deep inequalities. Not only are they pervasive, but they affect men's initial chances in life; yet they cannot possibly be justified by an appeal to the notions of merit or desert. (7; 7 Rev.)

Inequalities are ok if there is equality of opportunity.

It is perfectly natural to believe that if Bob works harder than Andrea, he merits or deserves a greater reward for his efforts, other things being equal. This is because, for the most part, we want to hold people responsible for the choices they make: if Andrea chooses to work less hard, her rewards should reflect her choice. Merit and desert do not apply, however, to the case where Bob receives greater rewards simply because he is born to nobility and Andrea to peasantry. These sorts of rewards are not due to any merit or desert on Bob's part: they are simply an upshot of the fact that his society happens to have a particular sort of basic structure, and that he happens to have been born to a favorable position within that basic structure.

It may seem we are belaboring an obvious point here, but some readers have taken Rawls to be making a much stronger claim than he really intends. In particular, some have thought Rawls to be saying that how well our lives go is *entirely* determined by the basic structure of our society, and thus that any talk about individual merit or desert is meaningless. Nothing could be further from the truth, as we shall see later on. His point is only that the basic structure clearly has *some* influence, and that whatever influence it does have lies beyond the scope of individual merit or desert. Since the basic structure of society affects our life prospects in ways that we cannot plausibly be held responsible for, it is especially important that we get the basic structure right. Unjust institutions like slavery and sex inequality condemn millions of people to live lives significantly worse than they otherwise deserve. So which basic structure is the right one? That, as Rawls puts it, is the subject of social justice.

Rawls's focus on the basic structure has the effect of narrowing the scope of his discussion in a number of respects. One aspect of this narrowing, which we noted in Chapter 2, is usually implied rather than expressed in the text. Utilitarianism is sometimes interpreted as a comprehensive moral philosophy, indicating not only which basic structures are better than others, but also which lines of personal conduct are better than others. Rawls's focus on the basic structure limits our topic to the question of social justice alone.

In addition to this, however, Rawls explicitly notes two further limitations on his discussion in § 2. First, he observes that there are many institutions and practices of a larger or smaller scale than those constituting the basic structure of a society. For example, the practices of clubs or other private associations are on a smaller scale, and the practices of international relations are on a larger scale. Although Rawls considers some of these issues briefly in *A Theory of Justice* (and also, in greater detail, in some later writings), the main line of argument sets them aside so as to focus on the major institutions and practices of a single society, "conceived for the time being as a closed system isolated from other societies" (8; 7 Rev.). Further, he cautions that whatever the best account of justice with respect to societies turns out to be, it may not be best when applied in these larger or smaller settings.

The second limitation concerns the difference between what he terms "strict compliance" versus "partial compliance" theories (8–9; 7–8 Rev.). Strict compliance theories address how the basic structure of society should assign the benefits and burdens of cooperation on the assumption that everyone more or less does what they are supposed to do—for example, no one engages in theft, bribery, and so forth. Obviously, there will be some of this in any real society, and we would want the distribution of benefits and burdens to be adjusted accordingly: perpetrators should be punished, victims should be compensated, and so on. Partial compliance theories address these sorts of *ex post* adjustments. Rawls, however, restricts his focus to strict compliance theories, and this has prompted many readers to complain that his theory is unrealistic. From one point of view that is certainly true, but nevertheless there is another sense in which strict compliance theories must have a certain logical priority over partial compliance theories. To determine whether a particular piece of property was stolen, say, we must first establish who is its rightful owner—that is, who would have possession assuming that no one broke the rules in the first place. This is precisely the job of a strict compliance theory. Thus it makes perfect sense to begin with strict compliance, as Rawls does, and leave the problem of partial compliance for another time.

Having set out these basic definitions and restrictions, Rawls proceeds in § 3 to present "the main idea" of his particular theory of social justice, which he terms "justice as fairness."

Justice as fairness

... generalizes and carries to a higher level of abstraction the familiar theory of the social contract as found, say, in Locke, Rousseau, and Kant. In order to do this we are not to think of the original contract as one to enter a particular society or to set up a particular form of government. Rather, the guiding idea is that the principles of justice for the basic structure are the object of the original agreement. They are the principles that free and rational persons concerned to further their own interests would accept in an initial position of equality as defining the fundamental terms of their association. (11; 10 Rev.)

In Chapter 2, we discussed how justice as fairness captures the spirit of the traditional social contract view, while avoiding its difficulties. Roughly speaking, we are to imagine a group of rational persons situated in an "original position" behind a "veil of ignorance." The veil of ignorance places these individuals on an equal footing with one another and ensures that they will each arrive at judgments from a suitably impartial point of view. We then aim to deduce what "principles of justice for the basic structure" such persons would agree on: these are general principles for assessing the extent to which different configurations of social institutions and practice can be regarded as just or unjust. In other words, if we want to know whether slavery is just or unjust, we are supposed to ask whether it would conform to the general principles of social justice that rational persons in an original position behind a veil of ignorance would have selected for the society in which they are going to live out their lives.

Rawls is very careful to insist that the question is a hypothetical one—that the original position is strictly a thought experiment. "No society can, of course, be a scheme of cooperation which men enter voluntarily in a literal sense," he admits; "each person finds himself placed at birth in some particular position in some particular society." This was one of the objections to the traditional social contract doctrine. Even a society that is perfectly just on Rawls's own account will not *literally* be voluntary for most people. (We might interpret his earlier assumption of a "closed" and "isolated" social system as emphasizing this point, since the members of a closed and isolated society by definition cannot voluntarily withdraw their membership.) But it will have one extremely important and valuable feature that other societies will not have. Namely, in a society that is just in Rawls's sense, citizens "can say to one another that they are cooperating on terms to which they would agree if they were free and equal persons whose relations with respect to one another were fair." Thus, "a society satisfying the principles of justice as fairness comes as close as a society can to being a voluntary scheme" (13; 12 Rev.). This passage clearly evokes Rousseau's famous expression from *The Social Contract* that in a voluntaristic society, despite "uniting with all" in a shared system of laws and institutions, in a sense each person "obeys only himself and remains as free as before" (1762: 148). It is an extremely powerful and compelling idea. At the same time, we must admit that there is something of an ambiguity here, which Rawls never fully addresses. If the social contract is merely "an expository device," as Rawls later puts it (21; 19 Rev.), which we never literally have an opportunity to accept or reject, how can it transform us into genuinely free and equal citizens? This is a deep and difficult question, best set aside for another occasion.

What would we expect rational persons in an original position behind a veil of ignorance to agree on? The main body of

A Theory of Justice attempts to answer this complicated question in exceptional detail. But Rawls sums up the gist of his answer in § 3. Roughly speaking, he argues that rational persons would reject utilitarianism in an original position behind a veil of ignorance. "Offhand it hardly seems likely," he suggests, "that persons who view themselves as equals" (as the veil of ignorance compels them to do) "would agree to a principle which may require lesser life prospects for some simply for the sake of a greater sum of advantages enjoyed by others." This is because "a rational man would not accept a basic structure merely because it maximized the algebraic sum of advantages irrespective of its permanent effects on his own basic rights and interests" (14; 13 Rev.). Or at any rate, this is what Rawls will try to demonstrate. If people would reject utilitarianism in the original position, what would they accept instead? Rawls believes they would agree on two principles of justice:

> . . . the first requires equality in the assignment of basic rights and duties, while the second holds that social and economic inequalities . . . are just only if they result in compensating benefits for everyone, and in particular for the least advantaged members of society. (14–15; 13 Rev.)

These are the famous "two principles of justice," which we will be hearing much more about later on. Why would these two principles be preferred to utilitarianism? Again foreshadowing the much more detailed argument that will come in Chapter 3, Rawls suggests that the two principles capture our sense that

> . . . since everyone's well-being depends on a scheme of cooperation without which no one could have a satisfactory life, the division of advantages should be such as to draw forth the willing cooperation of everyone taking part in it, including those less well situated. (15; 13 Rev.)

Here we neatly return to the thought with which we began, namely, the idea of society as a vast and complex system of cooperation for mutual benefit. In order for everyone to cooperate willingly, it is necessary that the terms of cooperation be regarded as fair on all sides, and according to Rawls the two principles of justice as fairness describe for us the conditions under which this would be the case.

Study questions

1. To what extent are we responsible for how well our lives go, and to what extent are our life prospects influenced by political and social factors beyond our personal control?
2. Is the vision of a perfectly voluntaristic society—a society in which we have chosen the terms of our mutual cooperation for ourselves—an appealing ideal? What are its limitations?

3.2 UTILITARIANISM AND INTUITIONISM (§§ 5–8)

Having presented a brief overview of his central argument for justice as fairness, Rawls proceeds in the remainder of chapter 1 to examine in somewhat greater detail the main rivals to his theory: §§ 5–6 address utilitarianism and §§ 7–8 intuitionism. (We will discuss § 4 and § 9, which concern some methodological questions, together in the following section.) Given the historical context in which he wrote, which we discussed in Chapter 1, it is perfectly understandable that he should select these two rivals for particular attention.

Rawls defines utilitarianism as the view that "society is rightly ordered, and therefore just, when its major institutions are arranged so as to achieve the greatest net balance of satisfaction summed over all the individuals belonging to it" (22; 20 Rev.). Note that this definition restricts the scope of utilitarianism to assessing the major institutions of society, that is, its basic structure. In other words, he usually means by "utilitarianism" the utilitarian theory of social justice specifically, and not utilitarianism the comprehensive moral philosophy. He then offers a number of observations on utilitarianism. These observations are not yet intended as objections—or at any rate, not at least until we have some plausible alternative to work with; their main point is rather to highlight some points of contrast with justice as fairness that will be important later on, once the main argument has further progressed.

Rawls's first observation relates to the internal structure of utilitarianism: it is, as he puts it, a "teleological" theory. A teleological theory is any theory in which "the good is defined independently from the right, and then the right is defined as that which maximizes the good" (24; 21–22 Rev.). For utilitarianism, the relevant good is happiness. It is supposed, on this view, that we have an independent conception of what it is for a person to live a more or less happy life (more on this shortly), and that we can therefore simply define something as right or just insofar as it tends to maximize happiness. There might be, of course, many other teleological theories as well. One example Rawls mentions is teleological perfectionism. Perfectionist theories start from a conception of the good as the realization of some specific form of human excellence—say, a kind of artistic achievement, or a life lived in accordance with God's will, or something else. Much as with utilitarianism, a perfectionist might then go on to judge things as better or worse insofar as they tend to maximize the realization of the preferred sort of excellence. At the time Rawls was writing, perfectionist theories were not generally popular, and he mentions them mainly for the sake of being thorough; since that time, however, there has been something of a renewed interest in perfectionism, and so it is worth taking note of his scattered comments on the subject.

Now one thing that is striking about teleological theories in general—and about utilitarian theories specifically—is that they can seem to embody a certain sort of rationality. Consider how we make decisions with respect to our own lives. Often we face choices between some small amount of happiness right away and a much greater amount of happiness in the future. (To keep things simple, let us suppose that the later happiness is greater even supposing we have taken into consideration the probability that we might die before experiencing the later happiness, and other such discounting factors.) When faced with such choices, most of us believe that the rational thing to do is to opt for the greater (future) happiness rather than the smaller (earlier) one. This is not to say that we always, or even often, actually act on this choice, but rather that when we go in for immediate gratification most of us would regard this as irrational. In making this sort of judgment, we are effectively regarding our happiness at each of the different moments in our lives as more or less equivalent. Rationality thus consists in opting for those choices that will tend to maximize our sum total happiness, counting the happiness of each future period (each of our future selves, so to speak) perfectly equally. Teleological theories like utilitarianism simply extend this reasoning from the individual to the social point of view. If individual rationality consists in summing the total happiness over a complete life, counting the happiness at each moment perfectly equally, then it stands to reason that social rationality should similarly consist in summing the total happiness over a complete society, counting the happiness of each of society's members perfectly equally. "The principles of choice for an association of men," on this view, "is interpreted as an extension of the principle of choice for one man. Social justice is the principle of rational prudence applied to an aggregate conception of the welfare of the group" (24; 21 Rev.).

Rawls's second observation regarding utilitarianism is related to the first, and indeed basically a consequence of it. All strictly teleological theories, he observes, are indifferent as a matter of principle to distribution. In other words, it does not matter, except indirectly, how happiness is distributed in a society, provided that the sum total happiness is as great as possible. *Who* in particular is happy is irrelevant. Of course, the distribution of happiness might matter indirectly—if, for example, lots of people suffered from serious envy. In such cases, when some people are much happier than others, this might further reduce the happiness of the latter. In a cultural environment prone to envy, it might be possible to increase the sum total happiness simply by reducing inequalities in the distribution of happiness. But in other cases, utilitarianism might lead to the opposite policy. Suppose there were a special group of people who experienced exquisite and insatiable pleasure from the consumption of goods. Since these "utility monsters" (as they are fancifully termed in the philosophical literature) convert consumption into happiness so much more efficiently than their fellows, we might find that allocating them the lion's share of material goods in society will maximize the sum total happiness experienced.[1]

True, all the other members of society will be less happy as a result, but on the utilitarian view, "there is no reason in principle why the greater gains of some should not compensate for the lesser losses of others" (26; 23 Rev.). This may seem as an implausible scenario, but it is less so than we might imagine. People often adjust their expectations to their circumstances. In a plutocratic society with a few superrich members and masses living in poverty, the latter might become accustomed to their lot and thus capable of a reasonable degree of happiness despite modest means, while the former become exquisitely happy super-hedonists: the sum total happiness could not then be improved by a more egalitarian distribution of material goods.

Rawls's theory, justice as fairness, will not be indifferent to distribution in this way, and thus it cannot define social justice as the mere maximization of some good. Recall that teleological theories characterize the good independently of the right, and then define the right as the maximization of the good. In Rawls's terminology, any theory rejecting one or both of these propositions is a "deontological theory." Justice as fairness, he says, is deontological "in the second way," that is, by rejecting the principle of maximization (30; 26 Rev.). We will later consider the extent to which it goes along with the first, which is a more complicated issue. In abandoning a teleological structure for his theory, Rawls forgoes the easy argument from rationality discussed above; his argument for justice as fairness will necessarily have a much different form.

Turning now to his third observation regarding utilitarianism, Rawls reminds his readers of the common intuition that individuals should have "an inviolability founded on justice or, as some say, on natural right, which even the welfare of every one else cannot override" (28; 24–25 Rev.). Thus, even if the sum total happiness could be increased by reintroducing slavery, or by locking up potential terrorists without trial, we should not do this because it would violate basic individual rights. Now while it is difficult for utilitarianism to account for these intuitions, as we earlier observed, it is not altogether impossible:

> Although the utilitarian recognizes that, strictly speaking, his doctrine conflicts with these sentiments of justice, he maintains that common sense precepts of justice and notions of natural right have a subordinate validity as secondary rules; they arise from the fact that under the conditions of civilized society there is a great social utility in following them for the most part and in permitting violations only under exceptional circumstances. Even the excessive zeal with which we are apt to affirm these precepts and to appeal to these rights is

itself granted a certain usefulness, since it counterbalances a natural human tendency to violate them in ways not sanctioned by utility. (28; 25 Rev.)

In other words, we might well imagine that locking people up without trial *usually* reduces sum total happiness. Thus, we introduce a rule of thumb, which simply states that everyone has a right to a fair trial. Obeying this simple rule is much easier than running all the calculations each time a new case arises, and the effort thus saved probably more than compensates for the few cases in which the rule actually misguides us. Indeed, convincing ourselves that the rule is *inviolable*, even if this is not strictly true, helps us adhere to it in moments of temporary passion or enthusiasm. This utilitarian argument for rights one might regard as more or less sound, except for a certain peculiarity: namely, that it accounts for rights only indirectly, as "a socially useful illusion" (28; 25 Rev.). This provides another point of contrast with justice as fairness, which will aim to account for rights directly, not merely as a useful fiction.

Rawls's final observation concerns the conception of happiness on which utilitarianism relies. This is an issue we have so far avoided, but it was in fact central to debates about and within the utilitarian tradition. Utilitarianism directs us to maximize the sum total happiness, but what counts as happiness? Broadly speaking, there were three different views. On the first, we say that a person's level of happiness is equal to the net of their pleasurable experiences, adjusted for intensity and duration, minus their painful experiences, similarly adjusted. Pleasure and pain are here taken to be naturalistic phenomena that, let us suppose, we could measure by connecting diodes to the correct areas of the brain. On this "hedonistic" view, often associated with Jeremy Bentham, utilitarianism instructs us to maximize pleasurable brain-states and minimize painful brain-states. The objection to hedonistic utilitarianism is that it suggests we should prefer a sedentary life plugged into a steady morphine drip to an experientially much richer, active life, with its usual emotional highs and lows. In order to get around this objection, J. S. Mill proposed a version of what might be called "perfectionist utilitarianism," according to which there would be an independent measure of the *quality* of various pleasures and pains as objectively

Mill proposed that some pleasure are measured better than others.

better or worse, independent of their *quantity*. Thus, we might claim, the single pleasure of reading a short poem by Lord Byron is objectively superior to the summed pleasures of enjoying many cold beers over a long, hot summer.

The various intricacies of this debate are complex, and need not concern us here. This is because, by the time Rawls was writing, both views had been abandoned in favor of a third, what might be called "preference utilitarianism." On this view, we simply define happiness as the satisfaction of preferences or desires, whatever the content of those preferences or desires happens to be. Thus, we say that Andrea is happier when more of her preferences have been met or satisfied, and less happy when fewer of them have. Notice that it does not matter on this view whether the satisfaction of a preference really generates a pleasurable brain-state or not; all that matters is that Andrea in fact had the relevant preference and that it was in fact met, one way or another. This preference-satisfaction account of happiness corresponds with the standard version of utility theory employed in modern economics and game theory, and it became the dominant school of utilitarian thinking as well. Rawls refers to it as "the principle of utility in its classical form" (25; 22 Rev.), and he attributes it to Bentham (perhaps inaccurately) and an important later utilitarian Henry Sidgwick, among others.

The relevance of all this for our discussion is that on the preference utilitarian account, we must remain strictly agnostic towards the content of a person's desires. "Thus if men take a certain pleasure in discriminating against one another, in subjecting others to a lesser liberty as a means of enhancing their self-respect," Rawls observes, "then the satisfaction of these desires must be weighted in our deliberations . . . along with other desires" (30–31; 27 Rev.). Thus, when aiming to maximize the sum total happiness, we must factor in the unhappiness that racists experience in not being permitted to discriminate against racial minorities. Of course, we hope and expect that this unhappiness will be outweighed by the happiness others would experience in not being discriminated against, but this cannot always be guaranteed. If there were enough racists in a given society, it might turn out that utilitarianism would permit discrimination. The general point here is that our rights, on a

utilitarian dispensation, will be sensitive to the contingent preference profile, so to speak, of the society in which we happen
to live. This will again be a point of contrast with justice as
fairness since, as we shall see, it fixes certain basic rights once
and for all, regardless of the prevailing preferences in society at
any given point in time.

To reiterate, although these may seem to be objections to
utilitarianism, they are simply observations at this stage. If there
were no compelling alternative, they would not in themselves be
sufficient to overthrow the utilitarian theory of social justice.
Each will, however, figure into the later discussion.

Rawls devotes §§ 7–8 to intuitionism. As we saw in the introduction, this was for some time the only available alternative
to utilitarianism. Rawls characterizes intuitionist theories as
having two main features. First, "they consist of a plurality of
first principles which may conflict to give contradictory direct-
ives in particular types of cases" (34; 30 Rev.). These first
principles might include basic precepts such as fidelity, bene-
volence, equity, and so forth, and we are supposed to be able to
apprehend them directly through the exercise of our common
sense intuitive moral judgment. Thus, for example, our sense
that Andrea should repay a loan from Bob despite the subsequent inconvenience of doing so suggests that fidelity is a
basic moral principle. The second main feature of intuitionist
theories is that "they include no explicit method, no priority
rules, for weighing these principles against one another: we
are simply to strike a balance by intuition, by what seems to us
most nearly right" (ibid.). Here we might imagine that Andrea
cannot repay Bob without depriving her son of a needed visit
to the doctor. Which should take priority, her fidelity to Bob
or her obligation to care for her son? Of course we may have
further intuitions here as well, but there is no general system
on the intuitionist theory for ranking or weighting of the basic
moral principles. Indeed, intuitionists often argued that no
such system exists, that "the complexity of the moral facts
defies our efforts to give a full account of our judgments" (39;
35 Rev.). Both these features of intuitionism pose challenges
for the theory, and partly account for its failure to displace
utilitarianism as the dominant tradition in moral and political
philosophy.

We have already discussed how the second feature generated what Rawls terms the "priority problem." The priority problem is especially pressing, he urges, when it comes to theories of social justice. Among the most important roles of a theory of social justice is its role in the resolution of disputes concerning the organization of the basic structure of society. When basic moral principles conflict, intuitionism would have us fall back on our intuitions regarding their relative rankings or weights. But many political conflicts arise precisely because people's intuitions diverge most strongly when it comes to such rankings. For example, most Americans value both equality and liberty to some extent, but disagree emphatically on which is more important or fundamental. Intuitionism provides no guidance in such cases. Utilitarianism solves the priority problem handily, by reducing all problems of social justice to a single metric—the maximization of sum total happiness. Justice as fairness will solve the priority problem in a different way: while admitting a plurality of basic principles, it will include in their specification a set of priority rules for resolving conflicts among them.

The first feature of intuitionism, however, is also a serious problem, as we shall discuss further in the next section.

Study questions
1. Should we be indifferent to the distribution of happiness in society? Does it matter that some people are made unhappy through no fault of their own, if their unhappiness permits the sum total happiness in society to be much greater?
2. Is there anything wrong with regarding our inviolable basic rights as a merely socially useful illusion?

3.3 REFLECTIVE EQUILIBRIUM AND METHOD (§§ 4, 9)
Intuitionism characteristically instructs us to discover basic moral facts through the exercise of our common sense intuitions regarding moral problems. There is, however, an obvious objection to this procedure. Where do our intuitions come from? As Rawls points out, "not only are our everyday ideas of justice influenced by our own situation, they are also strongly colored by custom and current expectation." Thus, we might reasonably want to know, "by what criteria are we to judge the justice of custom itself and the legitimacy of these expectations" (35–36;

31 Rev.)? How do we know that our intuitive judgments have not been clouded by a parochial upbringing?

This is a deep question in moral and political philosophy, and Rawls does not take it to be one of the main aims of *A Theory of Justice* to answer it in full. He does, however, more or less supply a sort of provisional answer. That his answer is only provisional should not be seen as an objection to his overall work: every argument, no matter how well constructed, must begin somewhere, and Rawls is at least explicit about this fact. Moreover, his provisional answer is, on the whole, quite sensible, and it is not clear that anyone else has a much better one. The relevant passages can mostly be found in § 4 and § 9, together with some remarks scattered throughout the remainder of the first chapter of his book; I bring these together here in order to better facilitate an appreciation of his overall strategy.

Often, as we have said, people have differing intuitions when it comes to moral and political problems, and even when people share similar intuitions, we cannot be certain that this is not merely the product of their having had similar life circumstances or experiences. Many people historically, for example, have had the strong intuition that women are inferior to men, but this does not demonstrate the validity of judgments based on these intuitions. How can we be sure that our present intuitions are not the product of similarly corrupt sources? Can we ever be certain that our moral intuitions are reliable? At some level, we cannot. But we can strive to work around this problem as best we can, and this is what Rawls sets out to do, at two different levels.

Our first strategy for working around the unreliability problem is to reduce as far as possible our dependence on bare moral intuitions. Utilitarianism provides a clear example of this strategy. Only three bare intuitions are required on that theory: first, that the happiness of individual persons is what ultimately matters; second, that a greater sum total happiness is always better than a smaller; and third, that the happiness of each individual person should count equally towards this sum. Utilitarianism then proceeds to dispense with all the other moral intuitions we might happen to have. On any possible question, we can in principle objectively determine the correct answer without consulting our intuitions: simply calculate which of the various options will tend to generate the greatest sum total happiness, counting the happiness of each person the same. When the result of this calculation (presuming we have carried it out correctly) conflicts with our moral intuitions in a given case, this demonstrates that those moral intuitions must be false— perhaps they are the vestige of some prejudice or superstition— and that they should be dispensed with accordingly.

Justice as fairness also strives to employ this first strategy, but in a very different and far more complex manner, through the device of the original position. Recall that the essential idea of justice as fairness is that the basic structure of society can be regarded as just insofar as it conforms to those principles rational people would agree to in an original position behind a veil of ignorance. Now we might ask, on what basis are people in the original position supposed to make their selection? In large part, the appeal of employing Rawls's procedure is that it seems capable of deriving moral conclusions from nonmoral premises. The genius of the wise judge's procedure for dividing the herd of cattle was precisely that it relied only on the rational self-interest of the two brothers in generating a fair outcome (see Chapter 2). Analogously, we can exclude moral considerations from the original position, and rely instead on the rational self-interest of the parties (constrained by a veil of ignorance) to generate a fair outcome. This has the desired effect of reducing drastically our reliance on bare moral intuitions. When it comes to some particular social institution or practice, for example, we need not consult our bare moral intuitions in order to determine its justness or unjustness. Instead, we can "ask whether, from the standpoint of a representative man" in the original position behind a veil of ignorance, "it would be rational to prefer this arrangement of the basic structure rather than that." Of course, this will not always be a simple procedure to follow, but in principle we will thereby "have asked a much more limited question and have substituted for an ethical judgment a judgment of rational prudence" (44; 39 Rev.). Much as with utilitarianism, conclusions derived in this manner might often conflict with our prior bare moral intuitions. This should lead us to question the provenance of the latter, which might have their origin in mere prejudice or custom. Suppose we have the prior intuition that women are inferior to men. From behind a veil of ignorance, however, not certain whether we were a man or a woman, it would be irrational for us to select principles of sexual discrimination. This shows that our prior intuition must be an unwarranted prejudice.

Rawls was probably thinking along these lines when he remarked, in a much maligned passage, that a "theory of justice is a part . . . of the theory of rational choice" (16; 15 Rev.). He found himself compelled to retract this statement in later writings, clarifying that he should have said the theory of rational choice is a device employed in a theory of justice (Rawls 2001, 82, n. 2). Nevertheless, it is undeniable that his method in *A Theory of Justice* involves a heavy reliance on the idea of rational self-interest. In order not to be misled by this, however, we must be careful to understand rational self-interest in a particularly broad sense. Consider, for example, two parties negotiating a simple business transaction. Now it might seem that the self-interest of each dictates that they aim to extract as many concessions from the other party as possible. However, both parties must also take into account the possibility that the contract might ultimately fail; thus, it would not benefit the stronger party to extract so many concessions from the weaker that the latter is almost certain to default down the road. Fully rational negotiators, presumably, would take such considerations into account. Rawls expects that fully rational people in an original position behind a veil of ignorance would likewise take broader, long-run considerations into account: when considering which principles of justice they should settle on in the original positions, the parties will consult more than their narrowest and most immediate interests.

What then are the relevant broader considerations? Rawls discussed them in the very first section of his book. For the most part, they flow from the various functions a conception of social justice is supposed to serve. Probably its most important function is to settle disputes concerning the organization of the basic structure in a society. Rawls expresses this thought by saying that a conception of social justice should be "public," by which he means that "everyone accepts and knows that the others accept the same principles of justice" (5; 4 Rev.). If the conception were not public, either because not everyone accepted it or because its principles were somehow concealed from them,

For issues (political) to be resolved everyone must accept the same principles of justice

it is difficult to see how it could serve as the basis for resolving real political disputes. Rawls defines a society as "well-ordered" when its basic structure more or less conforms to the principles of some conception of justice, and when that conception of justice is public, so defined (4–5; 4–5 Rev.). Prudential negotiating parties in the original position will certainly want their society to be well-ordered in this sense.

While publicity may be the most important consideration when choosing among candidate conceptions, Rawls admits several others, which again flow for the most part from the functions such conceptions are supposed to serve (6; 5–6 Rev.). First, the basic structure dictated by a conception of social justice must actually in some measure succeed in coordinating the plans and activities of society's various members. This usually entails setting up various reliable expectations such that ordinary people can plan out their lives. Second, the basic structure should to some extent be efficient in the achievement of desired social ends. By this Rawls presumably means that if the members of society desire some outcome, such as a robust level of economic growth, the basic structure should make it possible to realize this outcome as easily as possible—provided of course that this realization is consistent with social justice. Finally, the basic structure dictated by the conception should be stable in the sense that, once it is set up and running, it will tend to generate its own support. People born and raised under its auspices should find that they want to keep it going, rather than to resist and undermine it.

The original position procedure greatly aids in the process of moral reflection by reducing our dependence on unreliable, bare moral intuitions. But of course, as Rawls recognizes, we cannot eliminate such dependence entirely: "any conception of justice will have to rely on intuition to some degree" (41; 36 Rev.). This can be seen most clearly by posing the following question: If we want to claim that the correct principles of social justice are those that fully rational persons would agree to in an original position, how can we be certain that we have characterized the original position procedure correctly? This question is important because different parameters will tend to yield different results. If we permit the participants in the procedure to know their gender, for example, they might agree to different principles of social justice than they would if we did not permit access to this knowledge. We must then reflect on what *fair* conditions of negotiation would be. Unlike the reasoning employed by the participants themselves from within the original position, our own reasoning about the appropriate form of the original position will necessarily involve a reliance on at least a few moral intuitions. Must we then fall back on intuitionism after all?

Rawls offers his response to this challenge in § 9. Recall that one difficulty with depending heavily on our bare moral intuitions is that we cannot be certain these derive from reliable sources: they might merely be the product of prejudices or other biases. Our first strategy for responding to this uncertainty was to reduce our dependence by minimizing the role that bare moral intuitions play in constructing our theory. The original position procedure aims to do this, by replacing moral judgments with prudential judgments wherever possible. But this strategy cannot work comprehensively, because the design of the original position procedure itself must reflect certain moral judgments as to its fairness. Here Rawls introduces a second strategy—what he terms the method of "reflective equilibrium" (48–49; 42–43 Rev.). Suppose that we start with a bundle of moral intuitions on various topics, at various levels of detail and abstraction. Now we need not stop there, as the intuitionist does. Some of these intuitions are liable to be stronger or more deeply held than others. Rawls terms these "considered judgments"— namely, "those judgments in which our moral capacities are most likely to be displayed without distortion" (47; 42 Rev.). Suppose that we select a few of these more considered judgments, and then try to construct a theory—a theory of social justice—that would explain them in something like a systematic manner. Unless we get things exactly right on the first go, which is unlikely, our provisional theory will have all sorts of entailments that conflict with other moral intuitions we also have. Next, we examine one of these conflicts, and make a judgment as to whether we should adjust the theory if the intuition still seems compelling to us, or else drop the conflicting intuition if the adjustments required seem too costly to the overall theory. Proceeding thusly through all of our relevant moral intuitions, we eventually arrive at a theory we are happy with—that is, an internally consistent theory that sits well with all the intuitions we have decided, after careful reflection, to keep. This is a reflective equilibrium: the state "reached after a person has weighed various proposed conceptions" and then "either revised his judgments to accord with one of them or held fast to his initial convictions (and the corresponding conception)" (48; 43 Rev.). In § 4, Rawls basically demonstrates how the method of reflective equilibrium would be applied to the problem of determining the appropriate parameters for the original position (though of course, since this demonstration occurs earlier in the text, the underlying method is largely implicit). "In searching for the most favored description" of the original position, he writes, "we work from both ends" (20; 18 Rev.). He means by this that we start with two sets of intuitions. The first are intuitions about what sort of decision procedure would be fair. One intuition might be "that the parties in the original position are equal," in the sense that they "all have the same rights in the procedure for choosing principles; each can make proposals, submit reasons for their acceptance, and so on" (19; 17 Rev.). Another might be that "no one should be advantaged or disadvantaged by natural fortune or social circumstances in the choice of principles" (18; 16 Rev.). It would thus be unfair if the rich and powerful could manipulate the decision process so as to generate principles that would further enhance their already advantaged position. In addition to intuitions like these, Rawls also imagines that we have another bundle of intuitions about the nature of social justice. We have already encountered some of these, for example, our intuition that justice is more important than efficiency, and that people must have at least some inviolable rights. In a similar spirit, Rawls adds here the closely related intuition that "religious intolerance and racial discrimination are unjust" (19; 17 Rev.). Following the reflective equilibrium method, we should next design an original position that reflects our first bundle of intuitions, determine what sorts of principles of social justice it would generate, and note where these conflict with our second bundle of intuitions. Presuming that there will be such conflicts, we must then either adjust the design of the original position, modify our intuitions about social justice, or both, until the whole theory arrives at a reflective equilibrium.

Rawls does not actually narrate this process for us, of course. Rather, we are supposed to imagine that the method of reflective equilibrium has already been employed, and that what we have in *A Theory of Justice* is a detailed report as to its results. Thus the specific theory he presents us with is supposed to represent the view that best sits with all the intuitions we will, after careful reflection, decide to keep. (Some other intuitions, he admits much later in §§ 47–48, we will have to revise or dispense with.) We are certainly free to dispute his results, but then the burden falls on us to show that some other theory might better account for our considered judgments regarding social justice. It is not enough that we disagree with this or that minor point, or that we feel this or that conclusion is far-fetched. Rawls freely admits that "all theories," including his own, "are presumably mistaken in places. The real question at any given time is which of the views already proposed is the best approximation overall" (52; 45 Rev.).

Study questions
1. Must a theory of social justice be public in order for it to perform its distinctive function in society? Would it be irrational for people to agree on an esoteric theory that only a few know and understand?
2. Is it possible to dispense with intuitions in moral and political philosophy? If not, does the method of reflective equilibrium successfully address this problem?

3.4 THE TWO PRINCIPLES OF JUSTICE (§§ 10–14)
Let us briefly review where we stand at the end of the first chapter. The dominant theory of social justice has long been utilitarianism. According to this view, a just society is one in which the basic structure is configured so as to maximize the sum total happiness, counting everyone's happiness equally. Rawls wants to propose an alternative theory—what he calls justice as fairness. Broadly speaking, he now has two main tasks ahead of him. The first is to explain in greater detail what justice as fairness really amounts to. Since it is a much more complicated theory than utilitarianism, this will not be easy to do. The second is to demonstrate that justice as fairness is superior to utilitarianism. For Rawls, this boils down to showing that rational persons in an original position behind a veil of ignorance would select justice as fairness rather than utilitarianism.

These two tasks roughly correspond to the topics of the second and third chapters of *A Theory of Justice*, respectively. As always, it is helpful to keep this bird's eye view in mind, so as not to get lost in the details.

The second chapter of *A Theory of Justice* opens with a review and elaboration of some points we have already encountered. In § 10, Rawls restates the observation that the subject of social justice is the basic structure of society, and that the basic structure of society is the configuration of major social institutions and practices that together constitute the background or framework within which people live out their lives. Rawls notes that every society has a basic structure, and that we can always dream up some theory of social justice according to which that particular basic structure happens to be the best one. We might then say that mere "formal justice" consists in the "impartial and consistent administration of laws and institutions" according to that relevant supporting theory. Thus we can imagine a "slave or caste society" that is just in the formal sense when those institutions are "evenly and consistently administered" according to their own peculiar principles (58–59; 51 Rev.). Clearly, this is not the sort of justice we are interested in. What we should care about first and foremost is *substantive*, and not merely formal, justice. Justice as fairness and utilitarianism are both substantive theories.

After these prefatory remarks, Rawls plunges into the meat of the discussion: §§ 11–14 lay out the two principles that constitute justice as fairness, and describe in detail how they should be interpreted. These are among the most important and difficult passages in the entire book, and they demand a very careful reading.

3.4.1 Preliminary statement of the two principles

For reasons that will be explained shortly, justice as fairness is formulated slightly differently in the two editions of *A Theory of Justice*. Let us begin with the version that appears in the original edition:

> First: each person is to have an equal right to the most extensive basic liberty compatible with a similar liberty for others.

Second: social and economic inequalities are to be arranged so that they are both (a) reasonably expected to be to everyone's advantage, and (b) attached to positions and offices open to all. (60)

Recall that that these principles are intended to guide the design of major social institutions and practices, which constitute the basic structure of society. The first thing we should observe here is that, whereas utilitarianism relies on a single principle, justice as fairness employs two. It follows that, if justice as fairness is to avoid the priority problem plaguing intuitionism, these two principles must be reconciled in some way. Rawls, accordingly, arranges them "in a serial order with the first principle prior to the second" (61; 53 Rev.). Elsewhere, he describes this ordering as "lexical" (42; 37 Rev.). The idea of a lexical ordering will be familiar from the method of alphabetizing words: we begin by sorting according to first letter, then among the A's we sort by second letter, and so on. In this context, the serial or lexical ordering of the two principles means that we must always satisfy the first principle before moving on to the second. This can be illustrated as in Figure 3.1. Imagine that the numbers in each box here represent units of basic liberties, followed by units of other social and economic goods. Under basic structure I, we see that all citizens have both equal rights and equal shares of goods. Basic structure II would greatly enlarge both group's shares of goods, but at the same time would slightly reduce the basic liberties enjoyed by the members of Group A. Although this alternative would score better on the second principle, it is ruled out by the first, and is therefore not acceptable according to justice as fairness. This feature of justice

Citizens:	*Alternative Basic Structures*		
	I	**II**	**III**
Group A	10, 10	9, 25	10, 15
Group B	10, 10	11, 50	10, 20

Figure 3.1

as fairness is intended to capture our intuition that individuals should have some inviolable basic rights that cannot be overridden, even for the material benefit of society as a whole. In contrast with II, basic structure III preserves equal basic liberties; thus, in deciding between I and III we can move on to the second principle. Now in III, shares of goods are not equal, but everyone's share is greater than in was in I—that is, the inequality is to everyone's advantage. Thus, III is better than I by the second principle.

Rawls suggests that the two principles can be thought of as a special case or application of a more general conception of justice:

> All social values—liberty and opportunity, income and wealth, and the bases of self-respect—are to be distributed equally unless an unequal distribution of any, or all, of these values is to everyone's advantage. (62; 54 Rev.)

The thought here is that when it comes to the distribution of important things we all value, the default distribution should be an egalitarian one. This reflects the idea, perhaps, that if one person is to have more than another, this inequality ought to be justified somehow. Suppose that letting some people have more than others encourages a greater effort from all, and thus enhances everyone's prospects: in this case, the general conception would permit that inequality. The two principles of justice as fairness arise from the fact that (at least in societies like ours) departures from equal basic liberties turn out never to bring advantages to all, whereas departures from an equal distribution of other social and economic goods in some cases might, as we shall see later on. Since the bulk of *A Theory of Justice* refers to the more specific two-principle conception of justice as fairness, we can more or less leave aside the general conception.

Most of the complexities in interpreting justice as fairness relate to the second principle, which we shall discuss further below. Before turning to these, however, some comments on the first principle. Rawls altered the wording of the first principle several times after the initial publication of *A Theory of Justice* in 1971. In the revised edition, he says that "each person is to have an equal right to the most extensive *scheme of equal basic liberties* compatible with a similar *scheme of liberties* for others" (53 Rev., emphasis added). In his preface to the revised edition, Rawls explains that this revision was due to some criticisms raised by the legal philosopher H. L. A. Hart and others. Basically, the difficulty was that, on the first formulation, it seems to be implied that there is some generic good called "basic liberty," the equal distribution of which should be maximized. This was not what Rawls wanted to claim. Rather, by "basic liberty" he simply meant a familiar bundle of specific rights as given by a list like this:

> political liberty (the right to vote and to be eligible for public office) together with freedom of speech and assembly; liberty of conscience and freedom of thought; freedom of the person along with the right to hold (personal) property; and freedom from arbitrary arrest and seizure as defined by the rule of law. (61; 53 Rev., slightly amended)

As Hart observed, it is by no means clear that these various specific rights could be reduced to a single generic good called "basic liberty" (Hart 1973: 233–239). How are we supposed to compare the basic liberty units of a right to free speech with the basic liberty units of a right to freedom from arbitrary arrest, for example? Rawls agreed, and the substitution of "scheme of equal basic liberties" in the revised edition for "basic liberty" in the original was intended to eliminate this confusion. The scheme of equal basic liberties thus envisioned is a schedule of specific rights that fit together into a coherent bundle which can be granted equally to all citizens.

This did not, however, put the matter to rest. Even on the revised formulation, there is still the suggestion that schemes of basic liberties are bundles that can be quantifiably measured and thus compared with one another as bigger or smaller. The difficulty with this suggestion is twofold. First, if there is no single metric for comparing particular rights, how can there be a single metric for comparing bundles of rights? Doesn't the objection to the original formulation apply equally well to the revised one? Second, even supposing we can compare schemes of basic liberties according to their relative size or extensiveness, the directive that we choose the "most extensive scheme" would seem to preclude the need for a second principle of justice altogether. When considering any two basic structures, if there is any difference between them at all, this presumably will be reflected in at least some minor difference with respect to their schemes of basic liberties. Since the first principle has lexical priority over the second, we are therefore directed to select the more extensive scheme, and that is the end of the matter. The second principle of justice would never come up.

Rawls later cleared away these difficulties by revising the first principle a second time, to read "each person has an equal right to *a fully adequate* scheme of equal basic liberties which is compatible with a similar scheme of liberties for all" (Rawls 1993: 291, emphasis added). This was to be his definitive formulation of the first principle. The familiar list of basic liberties given above is taken to suggest what a "fully adequate" scheme would be like. Once we have supplied the rights thus enumerated to every citizen, the first principle of justice is satisfied, and we can move on to the second. This solution raises, of course, some issues of its own. Where is the particular list of basic rights supposed to come from? Why should these rights, and not others, count as fully adequate? And so on. In later writings Rawls attempts to address these questions (esp., Rawls 1993), but they need not concern us here. For the purpose of understanding *A Theory of Justice*, it is easiest to accept the enumerated list as a reasonably sensible one, and move on from there.

3.4.2 Interpretations of the second principle

The second principle of justice as fairness has two clauses, respectively requiring that any social and economic inequalities permitted by the basic structure be "to everyone's advantage" and "attached to positions and offices open to all" (60; 53 Rev.). Both these expressions are ambiguous, however, and thus the second principle is open to several plausible interpretations. Which interpretation is best? Rawls devotes considerable effort to addressing this question, especially in §§ 12–14. All told, three alternative interpretations are considered in detail, each of which specifies the two clauses somewhat differently, and Figure 3.2 indicates the order in which Rawls discusses them.[2] Some readers have regarded the discussion of these alternatives,

	Readings of the Two Clauses	
Interpretations of the Second Principle:	"to everyone's advantage"	"positions and offices open to all"
System of Natural Liberty	Principle of Efficiency	Formal Equality of Opportunity
Liberal Equality	Principle of Efficiency	Fair Equality of Opportunity
Democratic Equality	Difference Principle	Fair Equality of Opportunity

Figure 3.2

together with some remarks in § 17, as suggesting an independent line of argument for justice as fairness, in addition to the main argument (from the original position) later presented in the third chapter of *A Theory of Justice*. Rawls is clear, however, that this is not the case: "none of the . . . remarks" in these sections constitute an argument for justice as fairness, he says, "since in a contract theory all arguments, strictly speaking, are to be made in terms of what it would be rational to choose in the original position" (75; 65 Rev.).

But at the same time, recall (from our discussion of reflective equilibrium in Section 3.3) that we need some assurance we have designed the original position procedure itself correctly— that is, that our intuitive sense of fair procedures is itself reliable. Imagine, for example, that an initial design of the original position generates results significantly out of line with our intuitive sense of social justice: if this were the case, we would probably doubt the soundness our initial characterization of the procedure. Specific designs of the original position must be cross-checked, so to speak, with their respective results, and vice versa, until after an iterated process of revision and calibration we eventually arrive at reflective equilibrium. Accordingly, it is important that Rawls "prepare the way" by showing that his preferred interpretation of the second principle, which will ultimately be selected in the original position, does "not strike the reader as too eccentric or bizarre" (75; at 65 Rev. he says "extreme"). Far from constituting an independent line of argument, this preparation is part and parcel of the original position argument considered as a whole.

Rawls begins with what he imagines will be the most obvious interpretation of the second principle (at least, or especially, to his American readers). Referring to Figure 3.2, let us say that inequalities are to everyone's advantage when they satisfy what Rawls calls the "principle of efficiency," and that positions and offices are open to all when there is no discrimination on the basis of race, religion, gender, and so on—what is traditionally described as "careers open to talents," or formal equality of opportunity. Taken together, these describe what Rawls terms the "system of natural liberty" interpretation of the second principle (66; 56 Rev.). Rawls figures that the idea of formal equality of opportunity is clear enough to his readers, but he offers a lengthy digression meant to explain the principle of efficiency. Although this digression may be unnecessary for those familiar with the concept of Pareto efficiency in contemporary economics, for the benefit of the general reader we can explain the idea briefly as follows.

Economists generally define a distribution of goods as efficient if it is the case that no one can be made better off without making some other person or persons worse off. Suppose that Andrea and Bob are each given ten apples and ten oranges. As it happens, Andrea much prefers apples to oranges, but Bob likes them equally. Now imagine that Andrea offers to trade five of her oranges for four of Bob's apples. Since she likes apples better, she would prefer having nine pieces of fruit to ten provided that more of them were apples. Since Bob likes both the same, eleven pieces of fruit are better than ten for him. Thus the trade makes them both better off, and neither worse off. It follows that the initial distribution cannot be described as efficient in the economist's sense. But suppose you permit people perfect freedom to trade with one another as much as they like. On the assumption that people will always agree to trades that improve their position and never to trades that worsen it, we can easily see that once all the trading is done, we will have a perfectly efficient outcome.[3] Andrea and Bob will keep trading fruit until mutually beneficial trades are no longer possible. Of course, we would not necessarily expect this outcome to be an *equal* distribution: that all depends on how the trading goes, and on what initial assets or endowments each brings to the marketplace. But the second principle of justice permits

[handwritten margin note: Principle of Efficiency]

inequalities provided they can reasonably be expected to be to everyone's advantage, and on the system of natural liberty interpretation we are to regard efficient distributions, so understood, as satisfying this condition.

But what initial assets or endowments would people bring to the marketplace in a system of natural liberty? Here the other clause of the second principle may be relevant. The requirement that positions and offices be open to all under conditions of formal equality of opportunity excludes any discrimination on the basis of race, religion, gender, and so forth. Assuming that such barriers have been removed, we can say that participants in a system of natural liberty initially enter the marketplace with two main assets or endowments: namely, their natural talents and abilities, together with whatever goods and services happen to have been conferred on them by others as unearned gifts (here we are especially thinking of inherited wealth and the education and care provided by one's family). These might be called the participants' initial natural assets and initial social endowments, respectively. By now it should be clear that what Rawls refers to as the "system of natural liberty" is really the familiar libertarian ideal of a perfectly free market economy. Since this operates as something of a default ideal for many people, especially in the United States, it is perhaps understandable that Rawls should take it as his starting point in working out the best interpretation of the second principle. It is, however, an interpretation he proceeds to reject. Why so?

Many people have the intuition that it is fair to hold people responsible for the choices they make. Thus, if Andrea is hardworking and Bob lazy, it is only fair that Andrea should secure a greater share of rewards than Bob, other things being equal. Part of the appeal of perfectly free markets is precisely that they tend to reward greater efforts with greater rewards, as is only fair. The flip side of our usual notion of fairness, however, is that people should not be held responsible for things beyond their control. With a bit of reflection we should realize that market outcomes cannot always be described as fair in this sense. How well our lives go overall, even in a perfectly free market, is only partly due to our own efforts: it is also due in some part to our starting point on entering the market. Our starting points, in turn, are the product of cumulative historical contingencies beyond our personal control. Suppose that Andrea and Bob work equally hard in a perfectly free market system. Will they achieve an equal level of success? Not necessarily. Andrea may start out ahead if her parents worked harder than Bob's, and were thus able to afford a better education for Andrea. How well Andrea's parents did in turn might have been influenced by the fact that they faced unjust discrimination, without which they would have done *even better* than they actually did; or by the fact that *their* parents were lazy, and never developed their talents; and so on, back as far as we care to go. Thus, observes Rawls,

> the initial distribution of assets for any period of time . . . is the cumulative effect of prior distributions of natural assets— that is, natural talents and abilities—as these have been developed or left unrealized, and their use favored or disfavored over time by social circumstances and such chance contingencies as accident and good fortune. Intuitively, the most obvious injustice of the system of natural liberty is that it permits distributive shares to be improperly influenced by these factors so *arbitrary from a moral point of view*. (72; 62–63 Rev., emphasis added)

His point here is that we cannot plausibly hold people responsible for who their ancestors were, what they were like, or what circumstances they faced. These historical contingences are "arbitrary from a moral point of view" in the straightforward sense that we can neither say people deserve or do not deserve whatever benefits and burdens those contingencies give rise to here and now. The fact that our grandparents were wiped out in a flood or hurricane, say, might have some influence on how our lives go today, but this influence is clearly beyond the scope of our own personal moral responsibility.

This thought suggests a somewhat different interpretation of the second principle, what Rawls terms the "liberal equality" interpretation (see Figure 3.2). Suppose we retain the efficiency principle, but drop formal equality of opportunity, and replace it with a principle of "fair equality of opportunity." The idea here is that, in addition to protecting individuals against straightforward discrimination, we would introduce a universal public education system "designed to even out class barriers" and thus "mitigate the influence of social contingencies and natural fortune" left unaddressed in the system of natural liberty (73; 63 Rev.). People would then enter the marketplace with roughly similar initial social endowments, at which point an otherwise perfectly free market could take over. How well your life goes on this scheme still depends in part on your own personal effort, but individuals with roughly equivalent talent and motivation would have a roughly similar life chances, regardless of family background.

While this second interpretation may seem to have some things going for it, Rawls identifies two serious difficulties. One is that it will probably be impossible to completely even out class barriers so "long as the institution of the family exists" (74; 64 Rev., slightly amended). This is because there are many less tangible ways in which parents can influence their children's prospects for better or worse—say, by providing a more or less nurturing home environment for them. These sorts of influences children themselves, of course, cannot plausibly be held responsible for. Nevertheless, throughout *A Theory of Justice* Rawls insists that abolishing families as a social institution would be too high a price to pay to achieve perfectly fair equality of opportunity, though he never precisely states why. (In later writings, however, he suggests that abolishing families would be infeasible, insofar as we have no practicable alternative means of social reproduction; and also that it would to some extent fall afoul the first principle of justice as fairness, which among other things guarantees a right of private association: see Rawls 1997: 595–601.) We will thus have to live with an imperfect degree of fair equality of opportunity, and find some other method for mitigating any unfairness that, as a result, remains.

The other difficulty is that, even if the project of liberal equality succeeds on its own terms in leveling out initial social endowments, there are other important respects in which the distribution of social and economic goods generated by perfectly free markets cannot be considered fair. The benefits and burdens conferred on us by our ancestors are only one aspect of the initial assets and endowments we bring to the marketplace. The other aspect, mentioned above, is constituted by our natural talents and abilities. Much as in the case of social endowments, the initial "distribution of abilities and talents" is the product of what might be described, from the individual's point of view, as a "natural lottery" that is "arbitrary from a moral perspective" (74; 64 Rev.). Now of course, talents and abilities can be culti-vated or not, and this is something for which we *are* each individually responsible.[4] If Andrea and Bob have a roughly similar native talent for music, which Andrea cultivates but Bob does not, it is only fair that Andrea should reap greater rewards from her talent. This is not what Rawls is talking about here; we can assume that our efforts to cultivate our talents and abil-ities (through advanced education, job training, etc.) will take place within the market system, and that the resulting distri-bution of social and economic goods will rightly reflect such efforts at cultivation. The relevant issue is rather our *initial* natural assets—whatever native talents and abilities we are simply born with. If Andrea has a native talent for music and Bob does not, this is not something for which Bob can plausibly be held responsible. Our initial natural assets are neither deserved, nor undeserved: they simply are what they are. The only question is what, if anything, should be done about this fact?

3.4.3 The difference principle

Now it might seem that the line of reasoning Rawls has been following here must be heading in the direction of some sort of radical egalitarianism. How else can we correct, not only for different family histories, but also for good or bad luck in the natural lottery for talent? Given a commitment to preserving the institution of the family, the principle of fair equality of opportunity alone does not seem up to the task, and perhaps our only alternative is to equalize outcomes in some degree. But this is not what happens. Instead, Rawls suggests a different route.

Imagine a society with two main groups or classes. Members of the first and much larger "working class" have no especially distinctive talents and abilities beyond the norm, but members of the second and smaller "entrepreneurial class," each have some especially distinctive talent or ability. Now as we have seen, Rawls believes that no one is personally responsible for the native talents they happen to be born with—this is just a brute fact of nature. But if we distribute social and economic goods equally to everyone, on the view that the members of the entrepreneurial class do not after all deserve their distinctive talents and abilities, it follows that we cannot expect them to invest much time or effort in cultivating those distinctive talents and abilities, for such investments will bring them no additional rewards.[5] This may well be worse for everyone, the working class included. Suppose instead we allow the economic system to reward greater talent: in other words, we permit better musicians to earn more than worse ones, better software designers more than worse ones, and so forth. This would generate inequalities in the distribution of social and economic goods, but as Rawls observes, it may be that

> the greater expectations allowed to the entrepreneurs encourages them to do things which raise the long-term prospects of the laboring class. Their better prospects act as incentives so that the economic process is more efficient, innovation proceeds at a faster pace, and so on. Eventually the resulting material benefits spread throughout the system and to the least advantaged. (78; at 68 Rev., final sentence omitted)

This story should be familiar from basic economics. Rawls is careful to say that he "shall not consider how far these things are true" (ibid.)—that is, that is the job of expert economists to determine just how far incentives really do operate in this manner. But he assumes, as is very plausible, that this story is true at least to some extent. It follows that perfect equality will not always be to everyone's advantage, and indeed that permitting *some* degree of inequality might actually make everyone better off, because it would then be possible to offer people incentives to exploit whatever natural talents and abilities they happen to be born with. Everyone benefits, we might think, when we make the best possible use of the total pool of talent available to society.

How far should we permit this reasoning to extend? How great should we permit these inequalities to be? Rawls answers this question with what he calls the "difference principle," according to which "higher expectations of those better situated are just if and only if they work as part of a scheme which improves the expectations he least advantaged members of society" (75; 65 Rev.). The difference principle substitutes for the efficiency principle as an explanation of the "to everyone's

[margin note: Difference Principle]

advantage" clause in the second principle of justice as fairness. If we combine the difference principle with fair equality of opportunity, we get what Rawls calls the "democratic equality" interpretation of the second principle of justice (see Figure 3.2). This turns out to be Rawls's favored interpretation, and accordingly he devotes considerable effort to explaining the difference principle, as we shall do.

First off, we should note that the "least advantaged" are not supposed to be the least advantaged individuals, but rather the least advantaged group considered as a whole. Rawls clarifies this somewhat later, suggesting that we might roughly characterize the least advantaged as the representative or average person living below what is called the poverty line in the United States— that is, one half the median income and wealth (which can be taken as a rough proxy measure for the distribution of all relevant social and economic goods)—at any given time (97–98; 83–84 Rev.). A second elementary clarification was neglected by Rawls, however, thus confusing some of his earlier readers. This is that the least advantaged group should be understood as a relative designator, not a fixed one. In the example posed above, we might suppose that the "least advantaged" group must refer to the working class specifically. With this thought in mind, imagine that the numbers in Figure 3.3 represent expected shares of social and economic goods for the members of the two classes under three possible basic structures. Which basic structure satisfies the difference principle? The correct answer is the second, not the third. This is because the "least advantaged" group is not defined as the working class specifically—whose prospects would be greatest under III—or indeed any other group in particular. Rather, the term "least advantaged" refers to

	Alternative Basic Structures		
	I	II	III
Working class	10	15	18
Entrepreneurs	10	25	14

Figure 3.3

the least advantaged group *relative to a particular basic structure*. Thus, in III the entrepreneurs are the least advantaged group, whereas in II the working class are. The difference principle favors the basic structure II over III (and over I), because the least advantaged relative to that basic structure are better off than the least advantaged relative to the others. Rawls eliminated this ambiguity in his later writings (Rawls 2001: 69–70).

With these simpler clarifications out of the way, we can discuss the detailed and, to many readers, confusing technical notes Rawls offers on the difference principle in § 13 (76–78; 65–67 Rev.). These revolve around a series of figures which, taking some liberties, look something like Figures 3.4 and 3.5. What are we to make of these figures?

The rough idea is as follows. Suppose that x_1 represents the expected income of the better advantaged group and x_2 the expected income of the less advantaged group. At the origin point in these figures, each group is assumed to have the same (nonzero) income, representing perhaps a perfectly socialistic economy. Now suppose that we introduce some market-style economic reforms. What would we expect to happen? Basic economics suggests that the total wealth produced would increase, but that this increase would be distributed somewhat unequally—specifically, the better advantaged group would receive a somewhat larger share. In Figure 3.4 this is represented as moving rightward along the OP curve, which we see is below the 45° line extending out from the origin representing equal distributions. The OP curve represents the set of feasible economic systems. Introducing still more market reforms moves us further rightward along this curve: more total wealth is generated, but an increasing portion of it ends up in the hands of the

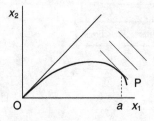

Figure 3.4

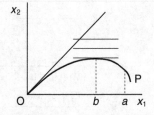

Figure 3.5

better advantaged. Where is the sum total wealth produced greatest? At point *a*, where the OP curve reaches as far to the north-east as possible. (It is possible for the better advantaged group to do better still for themselves, but beyond point *a* their marginal gains will be offset by greater losses to the less advantaged group.) We might imagine this represents the perfectly free market economy recommended by the efficiency principle. If individual happiness were simply a linear function of wealth, this is also the system utilitarianism would endorse. But the difference principle does not instruct us to optimize productivity: rather it instructs us to maximize the prospects of the least advantaged. In Figure 3.5, we see that this occurs at point *b* along the OP curve, representing, perhaps, a market-based economy combined with some social welfare programs. Although such a mixed economy will be less productive overall than a perfectly free market economy, further productivity gains cannot be achieved without reducing the prospects of the less advantaged. With some caveats, we might assume that Rawls intends to endorse something like this (he discusses the details later, in chapter 5).

Further questions may occur to some readers. For example, suppose we can improve the prospects of the better advantaged without worsening the prospects of the less advantaged. This would be equivalent, in Figure 3.4, to there being a flat segment along the OP curve to the right of point *b*. What does the difference principle tell us to do in such cases? We might think this is unlikely, insofar as economic relations in complex modern economies are, as Rawls puts it, "close-knit" (80; 70 Rev.): changes in the prospects for some are nearly always likely to have some effect on everyone else's prospects. If this condition does not hold, however, Rawls explains that the difference principle directs us to maximize the prospects of each group in society in ascending order. That is, we first maximize the prospects of the least advantaged; then we next maximize the prospects of the next-to-least advantaged, so far as this is consistent with not reducing the prospects of the least advantaged; and so on, up the scale until we reach the most advantaged group last (83; 72 Rev.). Given the plausibility of close-knitness, however, Rawls generally supposes that the simpler statement of the difference principle will suffice.

Another question we might have is whether the difference principle, which usually directs our attention to the least advantaged only, represents a plausible articulation of the "to everyone's advantage" clause in the second principle. Rawls argues that it does, provided that something called the "chain connection" generally obtains (80; 70 Rev.). The chain connection obtains when improvements in the prospects of the least advantaged (at least up to point *b* in Figure 3.4) are generally accompanied by improvements in the prospects of the other classes as well. Note that we are not *maximizing* the prospects of these other classes: it is certainly possible, and indeed likely, that they could do better still for themselves at the cost of *reducing* the prospects of the least advantaged. Nevertheless, the prospects of the other classes have been improved as against the baseline of a perfectly equal, socialistic economy. Provided that the chain connection holds, we might plausibly describe a distribution of social and economic goods satisfying the difference principle as being "to everyone's advantage."

3.4.4 Democratic equality and procedural justice

Having thus clarified the meaning of the difference principle, Rawls steps back and reflects on how the two parts of the democratic equality interpretation of the second principle of justice as fairness fit together. He does this by way of a very important, and often misunderstood, discussion of "procedural justice" in § 14.[6]

Rawls distinguishes three different sorts of procedural justice (85–86; 74–75 Rev.). The first is what he calls "perfect" procedural justice. This arises when we have an independent criterion for judging what a fair outcome or result would be, and also a method or procedure that infallibly generates precisely that result. The example he offers is giving the person who cuts a cake the last piece: this procedure reliably generates equal cake pieces, which is precisely what we think a fair division of a cake would be. Now contrast this procedure with that of a criminal trial. Here again, we have an independent criterion of what a fair outcome would be—namely, that the innocent are released and the guilty punished. The criminal trial system aims to achieve this result, but clearly it will not do so in every case; thus, it is an example of "imperfect" procedural justice. Obviously, as Rawls observes, perfect procedural justice is rare, and imperfect procedural justice the norm. What perfect and imperfect procedural justice have in common is that in both cases we have an independent criterion for assessing outcomes, and the procedure is simply a more or less reliable method for realizing those outcome. There are other scenarios in which we do not have such a criterion. Consider a poker game, for example. At the end of a poker match, the players will almost certainly have very different shares of chips than they had going in, but there is no independent criterion according to which we can judge these ending shares as correct or not—it is not as if Andrea should have ended the game with more chips than Bob, say. On the contrary (provided the rules were followed and no one cheated, of course), we would say that the outcome was fair *whatever the resulting distribution of chips happens to be*. This is what Rawls calls "pure" procedural justice. In cases of pure procedural justice, the procedure is not a (more or less reliable) method for realizing a fair outcome; rather, the very fact that the procedure has been followed is what *makes* the outcome fair.

Now let us consider the various interpretations of the second principle of justice as fairness in light of these distinctions. Reflecting on the natural liberty and liberal equality interpretations, we should see that each relies on pure procedural justice to some considerable degree. Neither advances an independent criterion for assessing what Andrea's share of social and economic goods should be relative to Bob's. Rather, each assumes there are certain rules—the rules of property and contract, for example—that together define a market system, and that Andrea and Bob are entitled to whatever shares they secure through their participation in that system, provided they follow the rules. By way of contrast, suppose we had a principle of distribution like this: "to each according to his or her needs." On this principle, we would have an independent criterion for assessing how large each person's share of social and economic goods should be. Thus, if Andrea had fewer needs than Bob, her share of goods should be less than his. This gives us a pattern against which we can assess the actual distribution. If, perchance, Andrea ends up with more goods than Bob, we would know this is not right: some of her goods should be reassigned to Bob. Robert Nozick, another Harvard philosopher contemporary with Rawls, called distributive principles that operate in this way "patterned" principles (Nozick 1974: 156). If you have a patterned distributive principle, you will undoubtedly need some method or procedure for generating the desired pattern: Rawls would describe this method as an instance of perfect or imperfect procedural justice, depending on the reliability with which the method maintained the desired pattern.

In moving from either the natural liberty or the liberal equality interpretations to the democratic equality interpretation, not only Nozick but many of Rawls's readers over the years have thought he abandons pure procedural justice in favor of a patterned distributive principle. After all, the difference principle tells us that the least advantaged should have as large a share of social and economic goods as possible, and this seems to give us an independent criterion for assessing actual distributions. The difficulty with patterned distributive principles is that it is impossible to maintain a pattern (and this is true regardless of which pattern your prefer) unless you are willing to continually interfere with people's basic liberties. Suppose you get the distribution between Andrea and Bob just right according to your preferred pattern, whatever that is. Moments later, they might voluntarily agree to exchange some of their goods. Thus, as Nozick observed, to "maintain a pattern one must either continually interfere to stop people from transferring resources as they wish to," or else periodically "take from some persons resources that others for some reason chose to transfer to them" in order to restore the pattern through coercive redistribution (Nozick 1974: 163). Either move would seem to violate some of our basic liberties.

Let us grant this difficulty. The issue is then whether the democratic equality interpretation of the second principle of justice as fairness really does embrace a patterned approach to distribution. Here it seems that Nozick and the others seem to have misunderstood § 14 of *A Theory of Justice*. Rawls is absolutely clear in that section that the second principle of justice as fairness, even on the democratic equality interpretation, is designed precisely "to insure that the system of cooperation is one of pure procedural justice" (87; 76 Rev.). How can this be? The confusion lies in assuming that the difference principle is meant to be applied directly to distributions of social and economic goods. This is not the case. The principles of justice, as Rawls stresses many times, are meant to apply to the basic structure of society—that is, to the design of society's major social institutions and practices. To continue with the poker game analogy, we are not supposed to use the difference principle to assess the outcomes of poker games, but rather their rules. The fairness of the outcome of a poker game crucially depends on the fairness of its rules: if the rules were designed to favor some players over others, we would say the game was fixed, and its results unfair. In order to achieve pure procedural justice, we must begin with fair rules or procedures.

Analogously, the basic structure of society constitutes the rules or procedures governing the "game of life." It follows that the shares of goods people end up with in real life can only be described as fair if the rules and procedures they are required to follow in the pursuit of their various activities are also fair. "Only against the background of a just basic structure," says Rawls, "including a just political constitution and a just arrangement of economic and social institutions, can one say that the requisite just procedure exists" (87; 76 Rev.). Consider, by way of illustration, two candidate systems of rules for an economic system. The first is the set of rules defining a pure free market economy; the second is identical to the first, except that there is a revenue-neutral negative income tax (this would proportionally tax incomes above a certain threshold and issue proportional tax credits of equal value below the threshold, less administrative costs). The second set of rules does not, any more than the first, dictate a particular distribution of social and economic goods to specific persons—it does not say that Andrea should have this much relative to Bob, and so on. Under both, how much people end up with depends entirely on the choices they make, the sorts of lives they decide to live. So which set of rules is better? That is the relevant question.

According to Rawls, the difference principle is designed to tell us what the best rules—that is, the best configuration of the basic structure—would be. It directs us to compare the likely prospects of the least advantaged (whoever they might turn out to be) under one configuration of the basic structure with the likely prospects of the least advantaged under another, and select accordingly. Once the background rules are set up, we suppose that people will live out their own lives, according to their own designs, and we can then say that they are entitled to whatever shares of goods they end up with as a result. This is pure procedural justice. The "great practical advantage of pure procedural justice," Rawls affirms, "is that it is no longer necessary . . . to keep track of the endless variety of circumstances and the changing relative positions of particular persons" (87; 76 Rev., slightly amended). Thus we need not know much of anything about the very particular and circumstantial needs of Andrea vis-à-vis Bob, provided the rules are followed. This makes things much easier and, contrary to Nozick's view, does not require continual interferences with basic liberties.

Let us review where we stand after this lengthy exposition of justice as fairness. At the end of § 13, Rawls restates the second principle of justice, this time using the preferred "democratic equality" interpretation of the second principle (83; 72 Rev.). Combining this with his later formulations of the first principle (found, as we saw above, in his later writings), we get the following:

Justice as fairness requires that:
First, each person has an equal right to a fully adequate scheme of equal basic liberties which is compatible with a similar scheme of liberties for all.
Second, social and economic inequalities are to be arranged so that they are both (a) to the greatest benefit of the least advantaged and (b) attached to offices and positions open to all under conditions of fair equality of opportunity.

This is not his complete statement of justice as fairness, as we shall later see. One unresolved issue, for example, is the ranking of the two clauses in the second principle: at this juncture, Rawls merely notes that they too will be lexically ordered (89; 77 Rev.), without clearly specifying what that ordering will be. But this is the working version of justice as fairness that will carry us through the main argument in the next chapter of *A Theory of Justice*, and it is close enough to serve for most purposes.

In conclusion, it is perhaps worth reiterating a point observed earlier. Throughout these difficult sections (§§ 12–14), Rawls's aim has not been to present an argument for the democratic equality interpretation of the second principle, for this argument must necessarily (on his view of things) proceed through the original position. Rather, his aim has been to show that, after due reflection, the second principle of justice as fairness so interpreted does not radically diverge from our considered intuitions about social justice. It is our intuition that we should hold people responsible for their voluntary choices, but also that it is unfair when some to do better or worse than others for reasons beyond their control. While the ideal of fair equality of opportunity in large part captures these intuitions, realistically speaking it cannot be fully implemented, and thus it is supplemented by the difference principle. If Rawls has accomplished his aim, we should now be persuaded that the two clauses of the second principle, operating in tandem, offer a reasonably good approximation of our considered intuitions about social justice. What remains to be done, however, is to demonstrate (through the original position argument) that these bare intuitions are genuinely sound.

Study questions

1. Does the difference principle offer a sensible compromise between the importance of achieving fair equality of opportunity on the one hand, and the importance of preserving the institution of the family on the other?
2. To what extent does the democratic equality interpretation of the second principle implement a desirable system of pure procedural justice?

3.5 CHARACTERIZING JUSTICE AS FAIRNESS (§§ 15–17)

At the beginning of § 15, Rawls indicates that he has completed his explanation of the two principles of justice as fairness (90; 78 Rev.). Rather than move on to the original position argument, however, chapter 2 continues for another five sections. Two of these (§§ 18–19) are an addendum, discussing how justice as fairness—a theory of social justice—relates to our moral obligations as individuals; we will consider these sections later, in connection with chapter 6. But where does this leave §§ 15–17, if the exposition of justice as fairness is supposed to be complete, but the argument for justice as fairness has not yet begun? Rawls's elliptical remarks provide little guidance. One way to read these sections, however, is as providing a *description* of what sort of theory justice as fairness is—roughly parallel to §§ 5–6, which gave utilitarianism a comparable treatment. If this reading is correct, then Rawls's objective in this part of chapter 2 is to highlight the points of contrast between the competing theories.

Here we might recall from our earlier discussion some of the characteristic features of utilitarianism. To begin with, utilitarianism assumes that the only thing that matters, from a social justice point of view, is happiness—that is, the degrees to which individual persons are more or less happy. It follows, from the utilitarian point of view, that the other things we might care about, such as our enjoyment of basic liberties, must be given an instrumental justification. We must account for our intuition that some basic rights should be inviolable merely as a socially useful illusion. At the same time, utilitarianism is strictly speaking agnostic towards the contents of our preferences. It does not matter, for example, that some people are made happier by discriminating against others: this too must be factored into our calculations. Finally, as a strictly teleological theory, utilitarianism instructs us to maximize the sum total happiness without concern for its distribution in society. Who in particular is happy does not matter, provided that the sum total happiness is made as great as possible. Having laid out an alternative theory of social justice—justice as fairness—Rawls next sets about describing how his theory takes a very different view of these matters.

3.5.1 Primary goods

Utilitarianism, as we said, assumes that levels of happiness are the relevant data when selecting among alternative basic structures. This view is often called welfarism. Reflecting on justice as fairness for a moment, however, it is evident that it does not take this view, since the two principles of justice as fairness make no reference to levels of happiness. What then are the relevant data? In one sense, we already know the answer to this question: the first principle is concerned with basic liberties, and the second with other social and economic goods. In an earlier passage, Rawls noted that these will be termed "primary goods" (62; 54 Rev.). What has not been explained is why Rawls believes that primary goods, rather than happiness, should constitute the relevant metric for social justice. In § 15, he begins to develop his answer to this question.

First off, we should note that the precise list of primary goods varies somewhat across Rawls's writings. In the original 1971 edition of *A Theory of Justice*, the primary goods are said to include "rights and liberties, opportunities and powers, income and wealth" (92); the revised edition amends this to read "rights, liberties, and opportunities, and income and wealth" (79 Rev.). Both editions note that an additional primary good, unmentioned to this point, is "a sense of one's own worth" or self-respect (92; 79 Rev.). This good is discussed later, in § 67 of chapter 7, where it is clear that what Rawls really means is *the social basis* of self-respect, on the thought that society can after all only provide a *basis* for our respecting ourselves: we must do the rest on our own. In a paper published later, Rawls further revised the list to read:

(a) First, the basic liberties as given by a list . . . ;
(b) Second, freedom of movement and choice of occupation against a background of diverse opportunities;
(c) Third, powers and prerogatives of offices and positions of responsibility, particularly those in the main political and economic institutions;
(d) Fourth, income and wealth; and
(e) Finally, the social bases of self-respect. (Rawls 1982: 362–363)

In subsequent writings, this list remains essentially unchanged, and so we may take it to represent more or less his final view.

Rawls defines primary goods in general as things it would always be better to have more of rather than less, or put another way, things "which it is supposed a rational man wants whatever else he wants" (92; 79 Rev.). He postpones a detailed discussion of the primary goods until chapter 7, but the gist of the idea is this. People often disagree about what is important or valuable. Let us suppose that, given whatever a person happens to value, she formulates a plan of life for herself: this might be to become a great doctor, or to be a good Christian, or to dedicate her life to environmental conservation or whatever. From a certain very general point of view, we might then say that what is good for a person is whatever helps or enables her to succeed according to the particular plan of life she has chosen for herself. Since people have different life plans, different things will be good for them—each will develop, in other words, a different conception of the good for him or herself. This much seems obvious. Now the claim Rawls wants to make is this: that for some goods, no matter what your life plan happens to be, it simply turns out that it will always be rational for you to want more, rather than less, of those goods. The goods for which this is true we can term "primary goods." Of course, you may want some other (nonprimary) goods as well, and the importance of the primary goods relative to such other goods (and to each other) might vary considerably depending on your particular life plan and its distinctive conception of the good, but you will always want more primary goods rather than less, other things being equal.

Why should this be? Consider a possible contrary example—someone who wants to dedicate her life to charity. This person might value income and wealth much less than other people, but it would still benefit her to have more money rather than less: after all, she would then have more money to give to those in need! It follows that she should rationally prefer having more income and wealth rather than less, other things being equal, and this is simply what it means for income and wealth to count as primary goods. Or consider another example—someone whose life plan is to be and remain a dogmatic Christian. It may seem that this life plan will succeed best if he is not exposed to alternative points of view. Might he therefore prefer to have *less* freedom of religion rather than more? According to Rawls, the correct answer is no. This is because, on his view, we should rationally prefer that our life plans be based on full information: to preclude our ability to revise our plans in the light of new information would simply be irrational. It follows that even a dogmatic Christian should rationally prefer having more religious freedom rather than less, other things being equal. Thus religious freedom, like income and wealth, must count as a primary good. With larger shares of primary goods, Rawls concludes, people "can generally be assured of greater success in carrying out their intentions and in advancing their ends, whatever these ends may be," provided of course that they are going to be rational (92; 79 Rev.).[7]

Though this initial account seems plausible, we might wonder whether the list of primary goods offered (even after his later edits) is really complete—that is, whether there are not additional things it would be rational to want more of rather than less, regardless of one's life plan. In fact, there almost certainly are. Suppose, for example, that Andrea and Bob have equal shares of primary goods as so far defined, but that Bob is diabetic, and thus must devote some portion of his primary goods to securing a supply of insulin. Would we say that they are equally well off? Probably not. Some have therefore suggested that Rawls count a range of basic human functioning as a primary good along with the others (see esp. Sen 1980). Curiously, Rawls resisted this move. In the revised edition of *A Theory of Justice*, he inserted a paragraph waving away the difficulty as follows:

> I shall assume that everyone has physical needs and psychological capacities within the normal range, so that the questions of health care and mental capacity do not arise. Besides prematurely introducing matters that may take us beyond the theory of justice, the consideration of these hard cases can distract our moral perception by leading us to think of persons distant from us whose fate arouses pity and anxiety. The first problem of justice concerns the relations among those who in everyday course of things are full and active participants in society . . . . (83–84 Rev.)

Here he seems to suggest that we treat normal cases first, before moving on to more difficult abnormal cases. Understandably, this answer did not entirely satisfy many readers. In later writings, he suggests that the appropriate response to disabilities depends on empirical facts that would not be known in the original position, namely, "the prevalence and kinds of these misfortunes" and "the costs of treating them" (Rawls 1993: 184). It follows, he argues, that such issues must be set aside until after we have selected the principles of justice that are to regulate the basic structure of society; this is to say that these issues are beyond the scope of his work.

For the moment, let us assume that the list of primary goods is satisfactory. Now utilitarianism holds that what matters is happiness, whereas justice as fairness holds that what matters are shares of primary goods. Why is one view better than the other? On Rawls's account, this must be part and parcel of the broader question of why justice as fairness should be preferred to utilitarianism, and the official answer has to be supplied from the point of view of the original position. In other words, one aspect of the argument that rational persons in an original position behind a veil of ignorance would select justice as fairness over utilitarianism is going to be that they would select primary goods rather than happiness as the relevant metric for social justice. Anticipating his later argument a bit, Rawls suggests that one pragmatic reason they might do this is that primary goods are probably easier to measure than happiness. Recall that theories of social justice are supposed to resolve real political disputes—that is one part of their role in society. In effect, the primary goods represent:

> an agreement to compare men's situations solely by reference to things which it is assumed they all prefer more of. This seems the most feasible way to establish a publicly recognized objective measure, that is, a common measure that reasonable persons can accept. Whereas there cannot be a similar agreement on how to estimate happiness as defined, say, by men's success in executing their rational plans, much less on the intrinsic value of these plans. (95; 81 Rev.)

Rawls is getting ahead of himself here, however. For the time being his aim is merely to highlight the contrast between justice as fairness and utilitarianism.

What does a move from happiness to primary goods entail? Several things. If our only concern is happiness, we must account for the value of basic liberties, opportunities, and so forth indirectly. This is not the case with primary goods, which are each considered independently valuable in their own right. If we take maximizing happiness as our aim, then we must take into consideration the fact that people are made happy in different ways. If some people are made happy by discriminating against others, then this must be factored in, and equally weighed with the unhappiness such discrimination might cause. If some people— the plutocratic hedonists discussed earlier (in Section 3.2)— convert material goods into happiness very efficiently, then they should be given greater shares of those goods. And so on. In substituting primary goods for happiness, we in effect agree to ignore this sort of information: provided that everyone has a fair share of primary goods, we agree that the demands of social justice have been met. The primary goods, thus, represent a fundamentally different way of looking at the problem of social justice. To a considerable extent, they involve assigning to individuals the responsibility of finding their own happiness according to their own plans of life.

3.5.2 Justice and solidarity

Earlier we discussed the idea that society can be viewed as a system of cooperation characterized, not only by mutual benefit, but also by conflict of interest. Since different configurations of the basic structure will benefit the various groups in society to different degrees, we must have some public conception of social justice for reconciling these conflicting interests from an impartial vantage point. Utilitarianism proposes that conflicts of interest be reconciled by summing the expected happiness generated by each option, counting everyone's happiness equally, and selecting the one with the greatest total. In effect, this involves thinking of society as a single person who does not care which of her many parts happen to experience the happiness. Alternatively, we might say that utilitarianism involves regarding society

[margin note: U sees society as on impartial, but benevolent, external spectator]

from the viewpoint of a perfectly impartial, but benevolent, external spectator. "It is this spectator who is conceived as carrying out the required organization of the desires of all persons into one coherent system," Rawls reflects in an earlier passage. Being external to society, the spectator has no specific personal attachments to any of its members; rather, "separate individuals are thought of as so many lines along which rights and duties are to be assigned and scarce means of satisfaction allocated" in the detached process of social engineering (27; 24 Rev.). It may seem obvious, from this external point of view, that the rational policy must be to maximize the sum total good.

[margin note: In JoF society is viewed from the viewpoint of every member/citizen]

Justice as fairness proposes a very different method for reconciling conflicting interests concerning the basic structure of society. Rather than regarding society from the viewpoint of an impartial spectator, we regard it from the viewpoint of the citizens themselves, imagining that they have come together as equals and settled on principles of justice agreeable to all. Not being impartial spectators viewing their own society from the outside, so to speak, equal citizens certainly will not be indifferent to how the various things they value are distributed. This is reflected in the first principle of justice, which directs us to distribute basic liberties equally, even if an unequal distribution could generate a greater sum total. And while the second principle does permit inequalities in other socioeconomic goods, it does so only in so far as those inequalities are advantageous to everyone, even if this means that somewhat less total wealth will be produced overall. This makes justice as fairness a deontological theory, as Rawls defines that term (see Section 3.2). Since the two principles do not maximize anything, we cannot rely on the deceptively simple argument from rationality sometimes deployed on behalf of utilitarianism; the argument for justice as fairness will have to be more complicated and less direct.

Before turning to that argument in chapter 3, however, Rawls offers some further reflections on the character of justice as fairness in §§ 16–17. These begin with the observation that viewing social justice from the point of view of equal citizens involves identifying "certain positions as more basic than the others" in "providing an appropriate standpoint for judging the social system" (96; 82 Rev.). In other words, justice as fairness disregards as a matter of principle considerable information or data that might be relevant for other theories. In focusing on primary goods, for example, we effectively agree to ignore the extent to which a unit of those goods happens to make one person more or less happy than another: an individual's happiness, we are saying, is their own business. Further, when evaluating the distribution of primary goods, we do not consider the particular shares of particular people, but rather the typical shares of representative groups: citizens in the case of basic liberties, the least advantaged in the case of other social and economic goods. Nor is our focus on the shares of primary goods people end up with, but rather on the shares they start with, as determined by the basic structure of society. The role of social justice is only to ensure that our *starting positions* are fair. "Once these principles are satisfied," says Rawls, "other inequalities are allowed to arise from men's voluntary actions" (96; 82 Rev.). Here we see that justice as fairness has incorporated the idea of pure procedural justice, in contrast with utilitarianism. Somewhat earlier Rawls noted that "utilitarianism does not interpret the basic structure as a scheme of pure procedural justice." This is because "the utilitarian has, in principle anyway, an independent standard for judging all distributions, namely, whether they produce the greatest net balance of satisfaction" (89; 77 Rev.). In other words, given sufficient information about everyone's preferences, we ought to be able to calculate in advance the precise allocation of goods that will maximize the sum total happiness. Since there is no guarantee that people would voluntarily settle on this pattern themselves, maintaining it might require continual adjustments and interventions. The procedures we establish for accomplishing this would then exemplify either perfect or imperfect procedural justice, depending on their efficacy in generating the desired pattern. This represents an important difference between the theories according to Rawls.

Justice as fairness, in contrast with utilitarianism, focuses on the role of the basic structure in determining our starting positions: it reflects the thought that we cannot personally be said to deserve or not deserve our initial endowments. "The natural distribution" of talents and abilities "is neither just nor unjust; nor it is unjust that persons are born into society at some particular position" in the class hierarchy, says Rawls.

These are simply natural facts. What is just and unjust is the way that institutions deal with these facts. Aristocratic and caste societies [for example] are unjust because they make these contingencies the ascriptive basis for belonging to more or less enclosed and privileged social classes. The basic structure of these societies incorporates the arbitrariness found in nature. (102; 87–88 Rev.)

Since these natural facts are neither just nor unjust in themselves, the aim of justice as fairness is not to eliminate them. Rather, the aim is to arrange the basic structure "so that these contingencies work for the good of the least fortunate" (102; 87 Rev.). This is precisely the role of the second principle of justice, and in particular the difference principle. In the original 1971 version of the text, Rawls says that "the difference principle represents, in effect, an agreement to *regard the distribution of natural talents as a common asset* and to *share in the benefits of this distribution* whatever it turns out to be" (101, emphasis added). Now this expression is clearly open to misunderstanding. It might seem to suggest that he believes Andrea's native talent for music, say, belongs not to her but to society, and thus that she is not entitled to whatever she produces with that talent. This is not at all what Rawls means to say, and in the revised version of *A Theory of Justice* he tries to clarify the thought as follows: the "difference principle represents, in effect, an agreement to regard the distribution of natural talents as *in some respects* a common asset and to share in *the greater social and economic benefits made possible by the complementarities of this distribution*" (87 Rev., emphasis added). His point, still somewhat obscure in the revised text, is not that society owns the talents of its members, but rather that the happenstance of Andrea's talents being different from Bob's, and Bob's being different from Carl's, and so on, is itself something everyone can benefit from through cooperation. We all benefit, in other words, from the fact that society contains a diversity of people with a diversity talents and abilities; thus it seems only fair that some of the benefits filter down to the least advantaged individuals in particular. This is what the difference principle is supposed to ensure.

To put the point more broadly, justice as fairness involves regarding society as a sort of common enterprise in which we all agree to share some burdens and risks, but at the same time, we all agree to place definite limits on the extent of sharing that can be demanded of each. The latter thought is expressed especially in the first principle, the former in the second. The idea of society as a common enterprise is arguably one of the most important underlying assumptions in *A Theory of Justice*.

This concludes Rawls's description and characterization of justice as fairness. Since it is a much more complex theory of social justice than utilitarianism, it has required considerably more effort to explain and has embroiled us in many technical details along the way. This first task completed, however, Rawls is at long last ready to move on to his second main task: namely, presenting the argument that justice as fairness should be preferred to utilitarianism.

Study questions

1. Does Rawls's list of primary goods accurately capture the set of goods that a person should rationally want more of rather than less, regardless of his or her particular life plan or associated conception of the good?
2. Is it better to rely only on the limited information captured by primary goods in resolving disputes about justice, or is the degree of happiness a person can achieve with his or her share of primary goods also important?

3.6 THE ORIGINAL POSITION (§§ 20, 22, 24–25)

The original position argument for justice as fairness appears mainly in the third chapter of *A Theory of Justice*. Unfortunately, to an even greater extent than in the previous two chapters, Rawls does not present his argument in an order resembling its most natural sequence, and so we are more or less compelled to jump around in the text. Let us begin with the chapter's first section (§ 20), in which Rawls reviews the form that the argument for justice as fairness is supposed to take.

All societies must, of necessity, have a basic structure governing how its members' activities will be coordinated and how the various benefits and burdens of that cooperation will be distributed among them. Which basic structure is best? Unfortunately, since "no one can obtain everything he wants," people tend to disagree. "The absolutely best for any man," we might suppose, "is that everyone else should join with him in furthering his conception of the good whatever it turns out to be," but of course "other persons will never agree to such terms" (119; 103 Rev.). Some basic structures might forcibly be imposed on society for the benefit of this or that specially advantaged group, but surely we would not consider such a society just. Let us imagine instead that all the members of society get together and try to work out a set of mutually acceptable general principles—principles of social justice—that will guide the design of the basic structure for their society. Naturally, we would want the ensure that each of the participants in this assembly were sufficiently informed, that they considered the issues rationally, and that they negotiated on fair and equal terms with one another. These various procedural conditions, which we will discuss more fully below, are summed up in what Rawls calls the "original position." What sort of principles would people agree to in an original position? According to Rawls, they would reject utilitarianism and endorse justice as fairness. This demonstrates, in his view, that justice as fairness represents a better theory of social justice: it is the theory that free and equal citizens, given fair conditions for making such a choice, would choose for themselves. Thus, a society whose basic structure conforms to the principles of justice as fairness can be described, from a certain point of view, as a voluntaristic society. That is roughly how the argument for justice as fairness is supposed to go.

Now it is important to remember that the original position is only a thought experiment. We must not suppose that the success of the argument hinges on whether any actual group of persons has ever been—or could ever be—in something like a genuine original position. Rather, the original position argument represents an idealized model of a fair decision procedure. Rawls explicitly suggests a parallel here with the standard sorts of models we find in economics (119–120; 103 Rev.). Economic models begin with a set of simplified starting conditions and then, operating under the idealized assumption that all economic actors behave so as to maximize their personal welfare, derive conclusions about what, for example, equilibrium prices will

Answer to critic of OP as just a thought experiment & not a real life model.

turn out to be. Even when real prices in real markets do not conform to those predicted in the model, the model can prove extremely useful. It might, for example, help us understand why real prices are different from those the model predicts: perhaps some economic actors are behaving irrationally, or perhaps there are various market imperfections distorting prices. In roughly the same way, Rawls hopes to derive conclusions about the principles of social justice that rational persons would agree to in an original position. Even when real societies fail to conform to these principles, the original position model can help us understand why: perhaps the powerful have coercively imposed a basic structure on society, or perhaps people's judgments about justice have been inappropriately biased.

In carrying out this modeling exercise, Rawls believes that we "should strive for a kind of moral geometry with all the rigor which this name connotes." Of course, given the complexity of many moral and political problems, he admits that the actual discussion "will fall short of this," but nevertheless "it is essential to have in mind the ideal one would like to achieve" (121; 105 Rev.). Why does Rawls set deductive, geometric rigor as his ideal? Recall from our earlier discussion of intuitionism that we have important reasons for wanting to reduce as much as possible our dependence on unreliable, bare moral intuitions. The original position model strives to accomplish this by substituting prudential judgments (judgments about what rational persons would agree to in order to further their own interests) for moral judgments wherever possible. If we think of the original position model as a sort of computation machine that takes specified inputs and mechanistically converts them into principles of social justice, then we need only rely on two sorts of comparatively uncontroversial intuitions. The first are our intuitions about what negotiating conditions would be fair. The second are our considered judgments concerning what must be true of any acceptable theory of social justice—for example, on any acceptable theory, religious intolerance and racial discrimination must count as unjust if anything does. The idea is then to begin with what appear to be fair negotiating conditions, and see if the principles of social justice generated by the model so characterized match our considered judgments. If not, we slightly adjust the conditions, our judgments, or both, and repeat

Rawls believes one should always keep in mind the ideal society one wants to achieve even if it can't be done.

the exercise until eventually, after many such adjustments, we reach reflective equilibrium. To reiterate what was said earlier, Rawls does not actually narrate this lengthy process in his book, but rather reports on what he believes are its results.

3.6.1 The veil of ignorance

Let us begin, then, with our sense of fair negotiating conditions, that is, the conditions that characterize what Rawls calls an original position. "The idea of the original position," Rawls says, "is to set up a fair procedure so that any principles agreed to will be just" (136; 118 Rev.). What would have to be true of the original position for us to expect this relationship to hold? Suppose that some of the parties to the original position had the power to coerce the others into accepting principles condemning them to perform all of the unpleasant or dangerous labor in society. It might be rational when threatened at gunpoint, say, to acquiesce to such an agreement, but we would not, on account of this acquiescence, regard the agreement as just. This only goes to show what is obvious—namely, that negotiations cannot be considered fair when the use of coercive force is permitted. If the original position is supposed to model perfectly fair negotiating conditions, we must exclude the use of force. By similar reasoning, we must exclude deception: if some were allowed to deceive others, we would not have any reason to believe that the resulting agreement would necessarily represent justice. As Rawls puts it, if "the original position is to yield agreements that are just, the parties must be fairly situated and treated equally as moral persons" (141; 122 Rev.).

These two requirements are perfectly familiar from our usual sense of fair contract bargaining: no one believes that people should be held to contracts they agreed to only because they were coerced or deceived. Indeed, the exclusion of force and fraud are so obvious that Rawls hardly mentions them at all. Instead, he spends most of his time in § 24 discussing a further restriction, which he terms the "veil of ignorance." While this restriction may seem strange and unrealistic at first, it is important to appreciate that it is merely an extension of the same basic line of thinking. In imagining what rational persons would agree to *if* they were situated behind a veil of ignorance in an original position, we are merely asking ourselves what the likely outcome

[margin notes, handwritten:]
set up fair procedure to ensure fair result.

Negotiations not fair when coercive force used. & deception

veil of ignorance is an extension of this line of thinking - Agreements by rational people under fair conditions represents justice.

of negotiations would be *if* those negotiations were held under the fairest possible conditions. It makes sense to think that whatever fully rational persons would agree to under perfectly fair conditions must represent justice, if anything does.

So what then is the veil of ignorance? Rawls believes that deliberations about social justice will be as fair as possible when the participants do not know certain facts about themselves. Specifically, he says, we should imagine that "no one knows his place in society, his class position or social status." In other words, participants in the original position are not permitted to know whether they are rich or poor, black or white, a man or a woman, and so forth. Additionally, no one knows "his fortune in the distribution of natural assets and abilities"—that is, whether they are born with a talent for music, a gift for slugging home runs, or even whether they have any noteworthy special abilities at all. Third, no one knows "his conception of the good" or "the particulars of his rational plan of life"—whether he wants to become a talented doctor, a good Christian, a champion for the environment, or whatever. Note that we should include on this list not only unobjectionable conceptions of the good such as these, but also morally dubious ones. Some people, for example, derive pleasure from discriminating against and oppressing minorities, or women, or persons of differing religious faith. All societies have some such people, and so we must presume that they too will be present in the original position. But importantly, they will not be permitted to know that they have these sorts of preferences. Fourth and finally, the veil of ignorance prevents the participants from knowing "the particular circumstances of their own society. That is, they do not know its economic or political situation, or the level of civilization and culture it has been able to achieve" (137; 118 Rev.). Though Rawls does not specifically mention this, the relevant "particular circumstances" here include a knowledge of the distribution of conceptions of the good—that is, how many persons are committed Christians, how many are dedicated environmentalists, and so on.

Though perhaps puzzling at first, the rationale for each of these restrictions should be fairly clear after careful reflection. If I knew that I was white, or a man, I might bargain for principles that favor white people, or men; if I do not know these facts,

[handwritten margin note: Participant don't know certain facts about themselves in veil.]

[Handwritten margin notes: Force use to think about social justice from impartial point of view]

I have no reason to do so. The point of the veil of ignorance is thus to force us to think about the problem of social justice from an impartial point of view. The veil of ignorance implements, in a manner of speaking, the spirit of Kant's moral philosophy, which we discussed earlier (in Chapter 1). Rawls returns to this point later in his book, and so will we when the time comes.

At this stage, however, we might wonder the following: if so much information is hidden from the parties to the original position, what are their deliberations supposed to be about? It turns out there is plenty to discuss. Since the veil of ignorance hides only the knowledge of *particular* facts, we can infer that participants in the original position are fully aware of a great many relevant *general* facts. The first group of general facts Rawls discusses are what he terms "the circumstances of justice." On numerous earlier occasions, we have discussed the idea that society can be viewed as a system of mutual cooperation characterized both by conflict and identity of interests. As Rawls reminds us near the opening of § 22,

[Handwritten margin notes: Participants to know general facts ((Circumstances of justice) These are general facts about the world which generate conflict & identity of interests simultaneously in every society]

> There is an identity of interests since social cooperation makes possible a better life for all than any would have if each were to try to live solely by his own efforts. There is a conflict of interest since men are not indifferent as to how the greater benefits produced by their collaboration are distributed, for in order to pursue their ends, they each prefer a larger to a lesser share. (126; 109 Rev.)

Now the circumstances of justice are simply those general facts about the world which generate conflict and identity of interests simultaneously in every society.

Some of these facts are objective. Since human beings are always vulnerable to attack, it benefits everyone to band together for mutual defense. Since many worthwhile projects and endeavors require cooperation, it benefits everyone that we have some method for coordinating each person's efforts and activities. At the same time, alas, it is also a fact that land and natural resources are not so plentiful that everyone can have everything they desire. Thus we must decide how the various benefits and burdens of cooperation should be distributed.

The circumstances of justice also include some subjective facts, however. Even if it is the case that everyone benefits from social cooperation, different people "nevertheless have their own plans of life" which "lead them to have different ends and purposes, and to make conflicting claims on the natural and social resources available" (127; 110 Rev.). It is crucially important to appreciate here that Rawls is not claiming people are necessarily selfish or egoistic, always inclined to further their own advantage at the expense of others. Certainly this is true of some people, but that has nothing to do with the argument at hand. The point is rather only that people will inevitably have *different* life plans, based on their differing conceptions of the good. If one person aims to promote environmental conservation and another poverty relief, the two may well make competing claims to the same scarce resources, even though neither aims to advance her personal well-being at the expense of others. Even perfectly benevolent aims may conflict with one another. Thus we must include the subjective fact that people have differing, and potentially competing, conceptions of the good among the circumstances of justice.

Subjective fact that people have differing & competing conceptions of the good.

Since these are general and not particular facts about the nature of the human condition, Rawls tells us we can "assume that persons in the original position know that these circumstances of justice obtain" (128; 111 Rev.). In other words, although they do not know the particular characteristics of their own society, the parties to the original position do know that social cooperation in general is mutually beneficial. Although they do not know how well-favored their particular society is in terms of resources and development, they do know that the conditions of moderate scarcity necessarily apply. And although each participant does not know what his or her particular life plan or conception of the good happens to be, he or she does know that everyone has such a conception and that every society inevitably embraces a diversity of conceptions.

They know social cooperation in general is mutually beneficial

Scarcity

There are many other relevant general facts not hidden by the veil of ignorance. Indeed, "the parties are presumed to know whatever general facts affect the choice of the principles of justice" without limitation (137; 119 Rev.). For example, although the parties to the original position do not know their particular fortune in the natural lottery for talents or abilities, they do know

[handwritten top margin: They know people have diverse talents & their cultivation is very beneficial to society.]

[handwritten left margin: They have full access to economics, sociology, psychology, & natural science that might be relevant to their decision making.]

that human beings in general have many diverse talents and abilities and that societies as a whole can benefit when these are cultivated and their use is coordinated. Indeed, we should assume that the participants have full access to all the economics, sociology, psychology, and natural science that might be relevant to their decision making (158–159; 137 Rev.). If the distinction between what is known and what is not known in the original position seems at times arbitrary, we need only remind ourselves of the overall point of the modeling exercise. Our aim is to derive the best possible conception of social justice. In general, we should suppose that more information is better than less, except where that information is likely to bias the results. The role of the veil of ignorance is simply to screen out the latter sort of information while letting the former sort through.

3.6.2 The rationality of the parties

[handwritten left margin: Rational people that try to advance their own interests.]

So far, we have discussed only the conditions of negotiation in the original position. What about the negotiating parties themselves? What are we to imagine they are like? Here again, Rawls has us make a number of modeling assumptions, which he discusses primarily in §§ 22 and 25. The first is that we should assume "persons in the original position are rational," by which he means that in "choosing between principles each tries as best he can to advance his own interests" (142; passage deleted in Rev.). Now one thought here might be, how can they do this? If the parties to the original position do not know their particular conceptions of the good, how can they possibly know what will advance their interests and what will not? The answer, it turns out, conveniently matches up with the idea of primary goods, introduced earlier. Primary goods, recall, are simply defined as those things we can suppose a rational person would want no matter what her conception of the good turns out to be. Thus, even when situated in an original position behind a veil of ignorance, a rational person knows that she would

[handwritten left margin: More primary social goods than less.]

"prefer more primary social goods rather than less" (142; 123 Rev.). This is an excellent example of how Rawls has carefully ensured that the various parts of his theory neatly fit together and complement one another.

Given any two options, we should assume that people in an original position, even if they do not know their particular conception of the good, will always choose the option with more primary goods rather than less, other things being equal. This is the first thing Rawls means by "the rationality of the parties." He does not stop here, however: going further, he insists that we imagine the parties to be what might be called *strictly* rational. Strictly rational individuals are "mutually disinterested" in the sense that they "do not seek to confer benefits or to impose injuries on one another . . . . Put in terms of a game, we might say: they strive for as high an absolute score as possible," regardless of the scores of the other players (144; 125 Rev.). We can easily see the significance of this assumption with the help of Figure 3.6.

If we suppose Bob is rational, it is obvious that he will prefer option II to option I, since there is no difference between them except that both Andrea and Bob have larger bundles of primary goods in II. The more interesting question is whether Bob would prefer option III to option I. If he suffered from envy, he might not. In that case, he might accept a smaller bundle for himself, provided that Andrea does not have a bundle larger than he does. Rawls makes the assumption that a strictly "rational individual does not suffer from envy. He is not ready to accept a loss for himself if only others have less as well" (143; 124 Rev.). Now the flip side of envy is altruism. Would Bob prefer option IV to options II or III? If he were sufficiently altruistic, he might. In that case, he might accept a smaller bundle for himself so that Andrea could have a larger bundle. On Rawls's view, a strictly rational individual would not think in this way. Just as Bob should not accept a loss merely to prevent Andrea

	Shares of Primary Goods			
	I	II	III	IV
Andrea	10	15	20	25
Bob	10	15	15	10

Figure 3.6

from having more, so he should not accept a loss merely to ensure that Andrea has more. All he would care about is maximizing his own bundle of primary goods. In somewhat different language, we might say that Rawls assumes the parties to the original position will have only self-regarding, and not other-regarding, preferences.

Both parts of the mutual disinterest assumption strike many readers as problematic, though for opposite reasons: the exclusion of envy because, even if envy is irrational, it is unrealistic to assume that people do not experience it, and the exclusion of altruism because, even if many people are not often altruistic, surely being so is not irrational. So why does Rawls insist on mutual disinterest? It has nothing to do with his views about human nature. Rather, his insistence has strictly a methodological basis: "the postulate of mutual disinterest in the original position," he says, "is made to ensure that the principles of justice do not depend upon strong assumptions." We must remember that the original position model is supposed to reduce our dependence on unreliable, bare moral intuitions and thus avoid the difficulties that plagued intuitionism. So far as possible, we aim to derive moral conclusions from nonmoral premises, and this entails carefully excluding covert moral considerations from the model. "A conception of justice should not presuppose," as he puts it, "extensive ties of sentiment. At the basis of the theory, one tries to assume as little as possible" (129; 111–112 Rev.). In effect, we would be cheating in our derivation of social justice from the original position if we assumed that people in the original position were already moved by specific moral considerations. (It may seem strange to think of envy specifically as a moral consideration, but if permitted in the original position, it might for example lead the parties to place an unreasonably high value on equality for its own sake. Permitting altruism, somewhat more obviously, might lead the parties to accept unreasonably great personal sacrifices for the good of others, as we shall see in later discussion.)

Having explained the assumption of mutual disinterest, we must next observe that Rawls introduces two clarifications or, perhaps, qualifications. The first repeats a point made much earlier (in Section 3.3), that we must construe mutually disinterested rationality in a broad and long-run sense. Being strictly rational

[handwritten margin note: Must consider long term effect of adopting one conception of good over another.]

individuals, the parties to the original position must consider not only their immediate short-run gain, but also the likely longer-term effects of adopting one conception of social justice rather than another. This involves considering whether people are going to be able to stick to their agreement in the original position once the veil of ignorance has been lifted, and the principles of social justice implemented. From this point of view, the "general facts of human psychology and the principles of moral learning"—for instance, the extent to which real-world people (as distinct from the parties in the original position) are envious or altruistic—"are relevant matters for the parties to examine. If a conception of justice is unlikely to generate its own support, or lacks stability, this fact must not be overlooked" (145; 125 Rev.). Though a bit confusing at first, this clarification will prove important later on. While we are to assume that the parties in the original position *themselves* are neither envious nor altruistic, we *are* to assume that they take into consideration general psychological facts about the envy and altruism that *real* human beings tend to experience, and the conditions under which they tend to experience them. These general psychological facts might argue in favor of some principles rather than others, as we shall see.

The second clarification—arguably more of a qualification—is that we are to assume the parties to the original position represent not merely themselves, but also "continuing lines of claims," as for example the head of a household might care not only about his or her own share of primary goods, but also the shares of his or her descendents. This motivation, Rawls hastens to add, "need not . . . span in perpetuity," but we should assume that "their goodwill stretches over at least two generations" (128). For some complicated technical reasons connected with a later discussion of intergenerational justice, the revised edition of the text weakens this assumption by proposing an alternative requirement that "the parties agree to principles subject to the constraint that they wish all preceding generations to have followed the very same principles" (111 Rev.). This is unfortunate, because the centerpiece argument for justice as fairness actually relies on the earlier version of the assumption, which the revised edition of the text suggests is dispensable. More on this in due course.[8] For the time being, the main point is only

[handwritten margin note: This is generationally - at least two]

that we should assume the parties to the original position will want to advance their own aims, and the aims of their immediate descendents.

This completes Rawls's characterization of the original position, which he reviews at the end of § 25. While at first seeming perhaps strange and artificial, the original position is much less oo onoo ono goto uood to tho idoa. Indeed, from a certain point of view, we need not think of the original position as an assembly at all. Since people in the original position are prevented from knowing anything particular about themselves, Rawls observes, "there follows the very important consequence that the parties have no basis for bargaining in the usual sense" (139; 120 Rev.). That is, since no one can calculate that it would be to their particular advantage to adopt one set of principles rather than another, they have no basis for attempting to extract concessions from the others as a condition of agreement. The veil of ignorance, in effect, puts the participants on a perfectly equal footing: provided that each is strictly rational, we can expect that everyone will be moved by exactly the same arguments and will arrive at exactly the same conclusions—the "veil of ignorance make possible a unanimous choice of a particular conception of justice" (140; 121 Rev.). Thus, if we like, we can dispense with the metaphor of a general assembly of citizens and think of the original position as a point of view any one of us can adopt by ourselves at any time, simply by putting ourselves in the right frame of mind. To figure out what social justice is, we need only reflect on the principles of social justice we would choose for ourselves when we leave aside the particularities of our own position in society, and contemplate the problem from a strictly impartial point of view. The veil of ignorance is merely an aid for rendering this thought experiment more vivid and thus easier to perform. *Thought experiment.*

Study questions
1. What are the benefits and limitations of interpreting the social contract as a hypothetical modeling procedure?
2. Does Rawls draw a sensible line between information excluded by the veil of ignorance in the original position, and information not excluded?

3.7 THE PRESENTATION OF ALTERNATIVES (§§ 21, 23)

Now that Rawls has completed his characterization of the original position, the next step would seem to be "letting the model run," so to speak—that is, imagining some mutually disinterested rational persons behind a veil of ignorance, and deriving the principles of social justice their deliberations would generate. This is not quite how Rawls proceeds, however. Instead, he imagines that the parties to the original position are presented with a short list of specific candidate theories, and then simply asked which of these candidates they prefer. This means that his sights have been lowered: his argument, even if successful, will only show that justice as fairness is better than the listed alternatives, not that it is the best theory of social justice possible. Given that this, on his own admission, "is an unsatisfactory way to proceed" (123; 106 Rev.), we might wonder why he has opted for the more modest route.

His first suggestion is that the more comprehensive strategy would place too great a burden on the "intellectual powers" of the parties to the original position. Thus, "there is no assurance that the parties could make out the best option; the principles that would be most preferred might be overlooked" (122; 106 Rev.). But this is hardly convincing, given that we have already made a great many unrealistic assumptions about the parties' capacities. What harm could there be in one more? The better explanation lies not in the parties' limited intellectual powers, but rather in our own. Since *we* cannot imagine all possible conceptions of social justice, we cannot possibly implement the model in a fully satisfactory way. The best we can ever do is draw up a list of the various conceptions of justice we are presently familiar with, and subject these at least to the original position experiment. Naturally, it is always possible to add new conceptions to the list as we become aware of them, but in the meantime, the strongest result we can hope to generate is that justice as fairness is better than any of the known alternatives. Rawls, to his credit, is at least honest about this limitation. Given the historical context in which he wrote *A Theory of Justice*, it should be fairly obvious what the short list of alternatives must include: namely, justice as fairness, utilitarianism, and intuitionism. Given that utilitarianism was, at that time, widely regarded as the most powerful and compelling conception of social justice available, even the relatively modest conclusion that rational persons in an original position would prefer justice as fairness to utilitarianism is an exceptionally important result. Accordingly, achieving that result is the main burden Rawls shoulders in *A Theory of Justice*. It is not his only result, however, and so it is worth pausing to discuss the official list of alternatives in greater detail.

Rawls first proposes a list of alternatives in § 21. This list (as expected) includes justice as fairness, utilitarianism, and intuitionism, together with egoism and a few other possibilities we will discuss below. It will not be his final list, however. Somewhat later (in § 23) he introduces what he refers to as the "formal constraints" on acceptable conceptions of social justice, and these, it turns out, generate some adjustments to the list. What is Rawls up to here? His terminology is perhaps a bit misleading. One might suppose that "formal constraints" must be constraints on the form that a conception can take if it is going to count as conception of social justice at all. But this is not how Rawls explains the constraints. Rather:

> The propriety of these formal conditions is derived from the task of principles of right in adjusting the claims that persons make on their institutions and one another. If the principles of justice are to play their role, that of assigning basic rights and duties and determining the division of advantages, these requirements are natural enough. (131; 113 Rev.)

Recall from an earlier discussion (in Section 3.3) that the parties to the original position must consider not only their short-run advantages, but also their long-run interests, broadly understood. Some of the latter relate to the various functions that a conception of social justice is supposed to serve—most importantly, its role in settling actual disputes concerning the basic structure of society. It follows that the parties to the original position will simply rule out of court any candidate theories that could not possibly serve these necessary functions. (Interestingly, they will do so even if there is no veil of ignorance, since the considerations in question are relevant to everyone regardless of their particular social position.) If this is how we are supposed to interpret the formal constraints, then it seems Rawls is getting a bit ahead of himself, anticipating how deliberations in the original position will proceed before they have officially begun. But assuming the various formal constraints are indeed plausible, this bit of advance work greatly simplifies his later discussion by pruning the list of implausible alternatives, and by setting out constraints on the sorts of proposals and arguments that will realistically be admissible in the original position.

Rawls indicates there are five formal constraints on any acceptable principles of social justice. The first is that "principles should be general. That is, it must be possible to formulate them without the use of what would be intuitively recognized as proper names, or rigged definite descriptions" (131; 113 Rev.). The second is that the "principles are to be universal in application. They must hold for everyone in virtue of their being moral persons" (132; 114 Rev.). Though related, these constraints are distinct. For example, the principle 'everyone should serve Andrea's interests' is universal (everyone must follow the same rule) but not general (since it refers to Andrea in particular). By contrast, the principle that 'men should perform all the rewarding labor in society' is general (no particular persons are named) but not universal (since women presumably must follow a different rule). Given the veil of ignorance, of course, these constraints are redundant: it would be foolish of someone to advocate the principle "everyone should serve Andrea's interests" if they do not know whether they are Andrea or not. Similarly, no one would propose that men monopolize the best jobs if they did not know their gender. According to Rawls, however, generality and universality are not merely the likely upshot of deliberations behind a veil of ignorance but, more strongly, constraints on admissible conceptions of social justice in the first place. With respect to generality, he states that it is required if a conception is going to "be capable of serving as a public charter of a well-ordered society in perpetuity." This is because knowledge of the relevant principles of justice "must be open to individuals in any generation. Thus, to understand these principles should not require a knowledge of contingent particulars" (131–132; 114 Rev.). Now it is not clear his reasoning is sound here. The principles of hereditary monarchy, for example, would seem to fail generality (insofar as they include the specification of a named royal line), but nevertheless were perfectly capable historically of governing highly stable societies. With respect to universality, he merely states that its derivation "has a common basis" with that of generality (133; 115 Rev.). For similar reasons, we may doubt whether this is really the case. Fortunately for Rawls, nothing much hinges on the point, since the veil of ignorance will perform the required work in any case.

The third formal constraint is "publicity." This requirement constrains the parties in the original position to choose "principles for a public conception of justice" (133; 115 Rev.). In other words, they must envision a society in which everyone accepts and knows that the others accept the actual principles of justice that are governing their society. This rules out, for example, a scenario in which the parties to the original position agree to brainwash their future selves and their descendents such that they will not be aware of the true basis and justification for the basic structure that will govern their lives. Unlike the first two constraints, publicity does indeed flow naturally from our understanding of the distinctive role a conception of social justice is supposed to serve, for it is difficult to see how a conception could satisfactorily resolve real political disputes among citizens from whom it was kept secret. Rawls here adds the further observation that publicity seems to be implicit in any Kantian political or moral philosophy. For society to be in any sense a voluntary scheme, governed by principles citizens have chosen for themselves, they must surely be aware of the principles they have chosen.

Nor is there any difficulty with the fourth and fifth formal constraints. If a conception of social justice is to be effective in its distinctive role, it must obviously be capable of generating a complete and consistent rank ordering of feasible basic structures from best to worst. Rawls does not have a name for this fourth condition, but we might refer to it as an *efficacy* constraint. On similar grounds, any acceptable conception of social justice must observe "finality," in the sense that there "are no higher standards to which arguments in support of claims can be addressed; reasoning successfully from these principles is conclusive" (135; 116 Rev.). This fifth and last constraint would be violated, for example, by a principle that referred certain disputes regarding the basic structure to scriptural authority, that is, to a set of external criteria beyond the principles of social justice themselves.

Although Rawls does not explicitly say so here, efficacy and finality in effect rule out intuitionism as an acceptable conception of social justice. This we can infer from our previous discussion. Recall that one distinctive feature of intuitionism is that it embraces a plurality of independent moral principles. Since these principles might rank feasible basic structures differently, intuitionism will not generate a consistent ordering overall. Moreover, in resolving conflicts among its various principles, intuitionism distinctively refers us to our basic moral intuitions, which is to say, to an authority external to those principles themselves. Intuitionism simply cannot satisfy the functions required of a conception of social justice. It is thus no surprise that there is almost no further discussion of intuitionism in the text after its appearance on the list of alternatives in § 21; hereafter we should regard it as out of contention.

This leaves justice as fairness, utilitarianism, egoism, and a few others. Next we must observe several possible interpretations of egoism. On the one hand, we might mean by egoism some principle of justice like "everyone must serve my interests" or "everyone must follow the rules but me." But these sorts of first-person egoism are clearly ruled out by the generality and universality formal constraints. Even if we are not convinced by Rawls's claim that these requirements can be derived from the functional requirements of a workable conception of justice, nevertheless they will clearly not pass muster from behind a veil of ignorance. Since I do not know who I am in the original position, there is no way for me to ensure that I will turn out to be the person whose interests everyone must serve, or the person who gets to ignore the rules. What is not ruled out by the formal constraints, however, is the principle of general egoism, according to which "each person is allowed to do whatever, in his judgment, is most likely to further his own aims" (136; 117 Rev.). But it is not clear that this is a conception of social justice at all, insofar as it does nothing to resolve disputes or perform any of the other functions such a conception is supposed to serve. Rather, Rawls says, we should understand "general egoism as the no-agreement point. It is what the parties would be stuck with if they were unable to reach an understanding" at all (136; 118 Rev.).

General egoism, we should note, is not at all the same as libertarianism. Libertarianism would involve a positive agreement to respect and enforce some schedule of individual rights, together with the rules of a perfectly free market. That is to say, libertarianism is equivalent to justice as fairness on the "system of natural liberty" (rather than "democratic equality") interpretation of its second principle. Libertarianism does not appear on Rawls's official list of alternatives, but it should; its absence is best explained by his focus on defeating utilitarianism. Insofar as Rawls later presents arguments that will be effective against libertarianism, however, its inclusion will do no harm.

In order to complete the official list of alternatives presented to the parties in the original position, we need only two further additions. The first is perfectionism. Recall from our earlier discussions (in Section 3.2) that a teleological theory of justice is one that defines the good independently of the right, and the right as the maximization of the good. Utilitarianism is the teleological theory in which the good is defined as happiness, but if we define the good as the realization of some specific form of human excellence (artistic achievement, performing God's will, etc.), we get something else—a teleological perfectionist theory of social justice. Rawls groups all perfectionist theories under this heading with utilitarianism, though this is not strictly correct, since some perfectionist theories might reject the maximization principle. For example, a traditional theological conception might define social justice as the honoring of God's will through the strict observance of specified religious ordinances. This would give us a perfectionist, but nonteleological (i.e., deontological) conception. Nothing in Rawls's subsequent argument against perfectionism hinges on this point, however.

The final addition to our list consists of a family of what Rawls terms "mixed conceptions" (124; 107 Rev.). These are conceptions that mix-and-match different components from the theories already discussed. Obviously, we might imagine any number of such hybrids, but only one proves significant for the main line of argument that follows. This is a mixed conception in which we substitute the principle of utility for the second principle of justice as fairness. That is to say, on this mixed conception the basic structure should arrange social and economic inequalities so as to maximize the sum total happiness, subject to the requirement of the first principle that each person has an equal right to a fully adequate scheme of equal basic liberties.

Our final official schedule of alternative conceptions presented to the parties in the original position thus looks something like this:

1. Justice as fairness, on the democratic equality interpretation of the second principle.
2. Libertarianism (i.e., justice as fairness on the system of natural liberty interpretation of the second principle).
3. Utilitarianism.
4. Perfectionism (teleological or otherwise).
5. Mixed conceptions, including: the first principle of justice as fairness together with a principle of utility maximization in place of the second principle.

If the parties are unable to agree on one of these alternatives, they will be left with general egoism. The burden now facing Rawls is to demonstrate that mutually disinterested rational persons, situated behind a veil of ignorance in an original position, would select the first option rather than any of the others.

One further observation. Each of these alternatives is expressed so that it "holds unconditionally, that is, whatever the circumstances or state of society. None of the principles is contingent upon certain social or other conditions" (125; 108 Rev.). In other words, we do not find proposed conceptions like this: "justice as fairness if our society is economically developed, utilitarianism otherwise"; or "justice as fairness if our society is Protestant, perfectionism if it is Catholic, and utilitarianism otherwise." Why not permit conditional conceptions such as these? One obvious reason, Rawls notes, is that excluding such possibilities is necessary in order to keep the discussion reasonably simple. The deeper reason, however, is that a conditional conception is really an unconditional conception in disguise. Suppose we ask why justice as fairness is appropriate to developed societies, but not underdeveloped ones. Presumably, if the conditional conception has some nonarbitrary basis, there must be an answer at a higher level of generality. This might be, for example, because what really matters are individual's basic interests, and these are best served by justice as fairness in one context and utilitarianism in another. But that itself is really an unconditional conception, and so it should be added to our list with the others. The difficulty with conceptions expressed as bundles of contingencies is thus that they "conceal their proper basis" (125; 108 Rev.). What belongs to the list are conceptions specified in their direct and unconditional form.

Study questions

1. Is it fair to dismiss intuitionism on the grounds of efficacy and finality? Might some revised version of intuitionism serve as a workable conception of social justice?
2. Is the list of alternatives reasonably complete? What other significant conceptions of justice should be considered by the parties?

3.8 THE ARGUMENT FOR JUSTICE AS FAIRNESS (§§ 26–30, 33)

At long last, we arrive at the heart of the text—the official argument for the two principles of justice as fairness. Rawls begins, at the opening of § 26, with a brief informal line of reasoning that might naturally lead us towards something like justice as fairness. This sets the stage for the detailed demonstration that will follow.

Imagine a rational person in an original position behind a veil of ignorance. What sort of society would he choose to live in, if he did not know what his role in that society was going to be? Our first hunch might be that he must surely opt for a perfectly egalitarian society. His position is similar to that of the first son of the deceased cattle rancher described in Chapter 2—the son instructed to divide his father's herd of cattle into lots. Since the second son will simply choose the better lot if they are significantly different, the first son does best for himself by making the lots equally good. Similarly, not knowing what his role in society is going to be, a person in an original position cannot necessarily "expect more than an equal share in the division" of advantages; and since "it is not rational for him to agree to less" than an equal share, the apparently "sensible thing" for

	Alternative Basic Structures				
Citizens:	I	II	III	IV	V
Group A	10	21	28	36	39
Group B	10	17	22	25	21
Group C	10	14	15	14	10
Group D	10	12	13	11	8
Group E	10	11	12	9	5

Figure 3.7

him to do is to begin with a principle "requiring an equal distribution" (150; 130 Rev.).[9] But then consider Figure 3.7. Imagine that the numbers in each column represent the bundle of primary goods an average member in each group of citizens can expect to receive under several alternative basic structures; for the sake of argument, we can suppose that the five groups represent social classes of roughly equal size. Basic structure I represents perhaps a perfectly egalitarian, socialistic society. Would someone in the original position favor I over all of the other options? Maybe not. Compare this option with basic structure II, perhaps representing a broadly socialistic society into which some market-based reforms have been introduced. These reforms have encouraged entrepreneurial activity; as a result, although there are now some inequalities in the distribution of primary goods, most individuals expect larger bundles overall as compared with the perfectly egalitarian society. A strictly rational person—one who did not suffer from envy, say—in an original position behind a veil of ignorance would thus surely prefer II to I since, no matter which group turns out to be his, his expected bundle of primary goods will be larger overall. "If there are inequalities . . . that work to make everyone better off in comparison with the benchmark of initial equality," asks Rawls, "why not permit them?" (151; 130–131 Rev.). It can easily be seen that the same reasoning will lead rational people in an original position to prefer III to either II or I. Basic structure III represents perhaps a mixed capitalist society, with fairly robust social welfare programs and a progressive tax structure.

But next consider basic structure IV, representing perhaps a pure capitalist society, without any social welfare programs or progressive taxes. According to the standard economic theories we are familiar with, a pure capitalist society will be the most economically productive and prosperous society overall. Thus the sum total primary goods in column four is greater than that in any of the other columns. (Basic structure V perhaps represents a plutocratic society in which political and social institutions favor the wealthy as much as possible, further improving the position of the most advantaged, but yielding less productivity overall than pure capitalism.) If our aim were simply to maximize the sum total primary goods produced in society, then we would choose basic structure IV over III. But is this the aim people would adopt from the vantage point of the original position? According to Rawls, it is not. Notice that, although there are more goods produced overall in such a society, the least advantaged groups fair rather poorly; in fact, the bottom three-fifths of society do less well under basic structure IV than they would have under basic structure III. Thus Rawls believes it would be perfectly sensible in the original position to opt for III—namely, the basic structure which maximizes the prospects of the least advantaged group. This (very roughly) corresponds with the recommendation of justice as fairness.

These informal remarks, according to Rawls, suggest only that "the two principles are at least a plausible conception of justice. The question, though, is how one is to argue for them more systematically" (152; 132 Rev.). That is the burden of the second half of chapter 3, §§ 26–30. These sections are both the most important, and probably the most difficult, in the entire book. Part of the difficulty stems from the fact that, although this is not made clear in the text, the main line of argument really has two distinct phases, which the reader must tease apart him or herself. Another difficulty stems from the fact that confounded with the main line of argument is a distracting side discussion of the choice between what Rawls terms the "average" and the "classical" versions of utilitarianism. This side discussion, it turns out, is much less significant than Rawls believed. The following reconstruction will attempt to reduce these confusions, so as to present his main line of reasoning in its most persuasive and attractive light.

3.8.1 The argument from basic liberties

One way to think about Rawls's argument is to imagine a series of pairwise comparisons between justice as fairness on the one hand, and its various competitors (from the list of alternatives discussed earlier) on the other. If we run through each possible pairing on the list, and justice as fairness emerges the victor each time, then our argument will be complete, and justice as fairness will have won the day. The most important pairwise comparison, naturally, lies between justice as fairness and utilitarianism, and so Rawls begins there.

This first comparison hinges largely on the value of what Rawls has termed "basic liberties." These, we may recall, are imagined to be specified on a list that includes such things as the freedom of speech and assembly, religious freedom and the freedom of conscience, the freedom of the person, and so forth. Justice as fairness would grant equal basic liberties to everyone unconditionally, as specified in its first principle. Utilitarianism, by contrast, would not. This is not to say that in a society governed by utilitarianism there would be no such rights or freedoms; rather, it is only to say that our rights and freedoms would be conditional on the particular social and historical circumstances of our society. For example, under some circumstances it will turn out that the unhappiness of being made a slave is much greater than the happiness of owning slaves. If so, utilitarian institutions will protect our freedom from slavery. Or again, under some circumstances it might turn out that the pleasure some people derive from oppressing religious minorities is simply not great enough to compensate for the misery of those minorities in being oppressed. If so, utilitarian institutions will protect our freedom of religion. And so on. In a society governed by utilitarianism, citizens will enjoy specific rights and liberties to the extent that their institutionalization can be expected, given the particular social and historical circumstances of that society, to maximize the sum total happiness, but not otherwise.

The question before us, then, can be stated most clearly as follows: From the vantage point of the original position behind a veil of ignorance, which principles of justice would a strictly rational person prefer? The principles that guarantee equal basic liberties unconditionally (justice as fairness), or the principles that provide them to the extent that doing so can be expected to maximize the sum total happiness (utilitarianism)?

Since people in an original position behind a veil of ignorance do not know the particular circumstances of their society, nor their position in that society, they must view this as a problem of choice under uncertainty. Usually, the sensible method for dealing with uncertainty is to calculate expected gains and losses, and select the option with the greatest expected gains. For example, suppose we are given the choice between having $10 for certain, and having $1,000 with probability p and nothing otherwise. In this case, it would be rational to accept the gamble if $p > 10/1000$, or 0.01. This may not always be the best method, however. Specifically, Rawls argues, the more sensible method for dealing with certain special sorts of uncertainty is to maximize the minimum ("maximin")—that is, to select the option whose worst-case outcome is as good as possible. The difference between these methods can be illustrated with the aid of Figure 3.8. Suppose we expect each possible outcome to be equally likely, regardless of the option we choose. On the usual method for dealing with uncertainty, option A would seem to be best choice, because its expected gain $(50 + 14 - 10)/3 = \$18$ is greater than that of the other options. The maximin method, by contrast, would direct us to select option C, since its worst outcome (valued at $9) is better than the worst outcomes of option A (valued at –$10) or of option B (valued at $8). Essentially, maximin is a *risk minimizing* approach to uncertainty.

When should we employ this method, rather than the usual one? Rawls mentions three features or conditions of those scenarios in which the maximin method would be the more sensible approach: first, when we have little or no basis for estimating the

	Possible Outcomes (in $)		
Option A:	–10	14	50
Option B:	15	8	10
Option C:	9	10	10

Figure 3.8

probabilities associated with different outcomes; second, when we place little or no value on gains above the best minimum outcome we can guarantee; and third, when some of the possible bad outcomes are unacceptably bad. Rawls does not believe that all, or even most, situations of uncertainly have this specific character. What he does argue in § 26, however, is that "the original position manifests these features to the fullest possible degree" (153; at 133 Rev., he softens this to "a very high degree").[10]

Regarding the first condition, there are two sorts of uncertainty to consider. The first relates to the particular circumstances of your society. For example, it might be probable, though not certain, that your society is one in which slavery would not actually increase the sum total happiness. The second relates to your particular position in that society. If there is going to be slavery, there is some probability that you will turn out to be a slave, and some probability that you will not. Now according to Rawls, "the veil of ignorance excludes all . . . knowledge of likelihoods," and thus, the "parties have no basis for determining the probable nature of their society, or their place in it" (155; 134 Rev., slightly amended). Alas, this statement merely asserts what Rawls needs to demonstrate, and the demonstration in § 26 seems to be missing. Given the general social science knowledge permitted to them in the original position, why can't the parties estimate the relevant probabilities?

Later, in § 28, Rawls does offer some considerations, but they do little to support his contention. First, he suggests that in the absence of specific knowledge about the circumstances of your society, it is most reasonable to assign equal probability to all possibilities (168–169; 145–146 Rev.). But far from giving us a reason to employ the maximin method, this instead offers us a means for persisting with the usual method of calculating expected gains and losses in the absence of more detailed information; moreover, it would work to the advantage of justice as fairness only if the probability of the worst-case outcomes (ending up a slave) is in reality much smaller than an equal weighting of all probabilities would suggest. Second, Rawls points out that, since the parties in an original position do not know their particular conceptions of the good, they cannot say how they would comparatively evaluate their unhappiness at being a slave, say, relative to their happiness at not being a slave; thus, the expected values of the various outcomes to be considered are not defined (173–175; 150–152 Rev.). But this suggestion is also puzzling, insofar as expected gains and losses can surely be calculated in terms of primary goods, which have been introduced precisely for use an original position where knowledge of one's particular conception of the good is not permitted.

With respect to the first condition, then, Rawls is not on his strongest ground. It is thus perhaps not surprising that the second and third conditions figure more prominently in subsequent presentations of the argument (e.g., Rawls 2001: 97–104). In *A Theory of Justice*, the argument relying on the latter two features is only vaguely sketched in § 26; much clearer is the discussion in § 33, which we can use here to clarify his underlying intuition. The second condition, recall, obtains when we place little or no value on gains above the best outcome we can achieve with certainty; and third when some of the possible bad outcomes are unacceptably bad. With respect to the second condition, justice as fairness secures equal basic liberties unconditionally for all through its first principle, regardless of the particular circumstances of society. This, we might sensibly believe, is not bad at all. Of course, by sacrificing the basic liberties of some, we might secure additional benefits (over and above the basic liberties) for others, but it is not obvious that these additional benefits would contribute much of value when compared with the great importance of the basic liberties themselves. Even more pertinent, however, are the grave dangers associated with opting for utilitarianism (now highlighting the third condition). Quite apart from the dreadful prospect of becoming a slave, recall that the parties to the original position are aware they hold particular conceptions of the good—that they have "moral, religious, or philosophical interests which they cannot put in jeopardy." They do not know what their particular conception of the good is, however, nor the distribution of such conceptions in their society—"whether, for example, it is in the majority or the minority" (206; 180–181 Rev.). Suppose we end up a Christian in a largely pagan society; the balance of preferences might be such as to favor (on utilitarian grounds) the oppression of Christians, which would be a disaster for us. Why assume this risk, given that we have the security provided by justice as fairness as an alternative? Indeed, according to Rawls, "to gamble in this way would show that one did not take one's religious or moral convictions seriously" (207; 181 Rev.).

Suppose a person in the original position were prepared to accept this danger, however, perhaps on the assumption that, more likely than not, he will end up in the majority after all. He must next consider the fact that the preference profile of society is liable to shift over time. In this respect, recall that the parties are assumed to care not only for their own interests, but also for those of their descendants; thus, any "choice of principles should seem reasonable to . . . their descendants, whose rights will be deeply affected" also by the decision in the original position (155; 134 Rev.). Even if our gambler finds himself a pagan in a pagan-majority society, this will be little comfort to his descendants when the balance of preferences later shifts in favor of the Christians. The parties to the original position, recall, must act as trustees for the interests of their descendants. Especially given that our gambler cannot be certain what the specific interests of his children and grandchildren are likely to be, it would be "irresponsible" of him not "to guarantee the rights of his descendants" (209; 183 Rev.).

In contrast with utilitarianism, justice as fairness fixes and settles equal basic liberties unconditionally, regardless of the particular circumstances of society now or in the future. Surely, Rawls believes, "the parties would prefer to secure their liberties straightway rather than have them depend upon what may be uncertain and speculative actuarial calculations" concerning the particular circumstances of their society. Even if we conjecture that the balance of preferences in society will *always* favor granting equal basic liberties on pragmatic utilitarian grounds, nevertheless

> there is a real advantage in persons' announcing to one another once and for all that . . . they do not wish that things had been different. Since in justice as fairness moral conceptions are public, the choice of the two principles is, in effect, such an announcement. (160–161; 138–139 Rev.)

That is, in opting for justice as fairness, we effectively announce as a society that we do not ever *want* the balance of preferences to shift in favor slavery, the oppression of religious minorities, and so on. This public announcement represents an agreement among the parties to permanently respect one another as equal citizens.

Many people have found the argument against utilitarianism from basic liberties extremely compelling. If we too are convinced, then Rawls has succeeded at his main task—that of demonstrating the superiority of justice as fairness over utilitarianism. In §§ 27–28 he aims to further expand and buttress his result, albeit through a muddled argument concerning the difference between what he terms "average" and "classical" utilitarianism. Since this aspect of the discussion adds little to his argument, we can be brief in our summary of its main points. Roughly, Rawls observes that the traditional formulation of utilitarianism, on which we have largely relied, is ambiguous at a certain point. This ambiguity, he believes, is highlighted in the original position. The issue is this: when we aim to maximize the sum total happiness, counting everyone's happiness the same, do we really mean the sum of the happiness of all the people who might possibly live? Suppose, for example, we face the choice between basic structure I, in which there will be ten persons who enjoy ten units of happiness each, and basic structure II, in which there will be twenty persons who enjoy six units of happiness each. From the vantage point of the original position, Rawls claims, we would surely prefer I to II, since ten units is surely better than six. If so, we are not really aiming to maximize the *sum total* happiness, which would be greater under II, but rather the *average* happiness.

As it happens, Rawls's reasoning is not perfectly sound here, unless we make an assumption we have no good reason to make—namely, that the parties to the original position are confident they are one of the ten people who will exist under either basic structure, and not one of the ten who will exist only under basic structure II. On what grounds should we assume this? Such questions raise complex problems relating to population policy, which are best left for our later discussion of intergenerational justice. For the time being, it is sufficient to observe that this issue is really beside the point, since in an original position, justice as fairness would be selected over utilitarianism on either of its possible formulations.

3.8.2 The strains of commitment argument

At this point, it seems Rawls can claim victory over utilitarianism. This was, after all, his main aim in writing *A Theory of Justice*. Some readers, however, might find they are disappointed. So far we have said nothing about the difference principle, for example, and it is precisely this aspect of justice as fairness that might have initially seemed most interesting and controversial.

To make matters worse, if we take the maximin argument offered in § 26 on behalf of justice as fairness, and endeavor to employ it on behalf of the second principle of justice in particular, our disappointment is bound to increase. The second principle of justice, recall, is designed to address the distribution of social and economic goods other than basic liberties. Given the full range of social science knowledge permitted in the original position, it is not difficult to imagine the parties constructing reasonable estimates of long-run income distributions, say, resulting from the selection of alternative economic systems. Moreover, unlike the value of basic liberties, the value of other social and economic goods varies more or less continuously over a considerable middle range. There is no specific threshold level such that more goods would add little of value on the one hand, but fewer would be calamitous on the other. We can imagine, of course, a fortune so great that many people would not care so much about having even more; and of course, a level of deprivation so severe that many people would avoid it at all costs. But between these distant extremes, the parties in the original position can probably assume that more social and economic goods are simply better than less. Given these observations, it is unlikely that the parties would resort to the maximin method of choice when it comes to their deliberations regarding the second principle of justice, unless perhaps we assume they are risk averse to an implausible degree (Barry 1973: 87–96; Roemer 1996: 175–182), and Rawls explicitly denies that his theory depends on any such psychological assumption (172; 149 Rev.).[11]

Where does this leave us? Perceptive readers may by now have realized that the argument is less a failure than it is simply incomplete. Here our earlier characterization of Rawls's argument as having several distinct steps, each consisting of a pairwise comparison between justice as fairness and one of its competitors, greatly aids our understanding. So far, we have considered only one comparison: that between justice as fairness and utilitarianism. That first phase in the argument having been completed, we can now move on to the second phase. This second phase is best characterized as a comparison between justice as fairness on the one hand, and either libertarianism or a mixed conception on the other (specifically, a mixed conception consisting of utilitarianism together with a basic liberty constraint). Notice that all the competing conceptions now share something like the first principle of justice as fairness, and thus all guarantee equal basic liberties unconditionally. It follows that none of the considerations advanced in the first phase of the argument will be relevant to the second. On the contrary, the argument in the second phase will necessarily hinge on the specific merits of the second principle of justice as fairness. The distinct argument for the second principle appears primarily in § 29, where Rawls makes no reference to the maximin argument relied on earlier.

It is not surprising that many readers have been misled with respect to the structure of Rawls's argument. First, it is not at all obvious in the text that the main argument really divides into two distinct phases. (In later writings, and indeed in the preface to the revised edition of *A Theory of Justice*, Rawls admits that the argument should have been presented in this manner.) Moreover, in the first phase, although the focus is on the importance of securing equal basic liberties, the discussion is never explicitly restricted to this topic (except in § 33), and indeed the mode of presentation frequently suggests that both principles of justice are under consideration together. Finally, and most confusing of all, the formal similarity between the maximin method of choice on the one hand, and the difference principle on the other (the one focusing on the worst case scenario when faced with uncertainty, the other on the prospects of the least advantaged members of society), virtually guarantees that the two will come to be strongly associated in the mind of any but the most astute reader—a brief warning against this mistake added to the revised edition notwithstanding (72 Rev.). Rawls endeavored to address these misconceptions in later presentations of the argument for justice as fairness (e.g., Rawls 2001: 94–97, 119–120).

How then does Rawls make his case for the second principle of justice as fairness? To begin, we must refer back to certain earlier assumptions about the rationality of the parties in the original position. Recall that strictly rational individuals would consider not only their immediate short-run gains or losses, but also the likely longer-term effects of adopting one conception of social justice rather than another. This involves considering whether people are going to be able to stick to an agreement made in the original position once the veil of ignorance has been lifted, and the principles of social justice implemented. Taking the long-run view, the parties "cannot enter into agreements that may have consequences they cannot accept," and thus they "will avoid those that they can adhere to only with great difficulty" (176; 153 Rev.). Rawls refers to these sorts of long-run considerations as the "strains of commitment." The idea is simply that, in comparing alternative conceptions of justice, the parties will not want the strains of commitment to be too great, insofar as this would raise the prospect of their agreement ultimately falling apart and their hard work in the original position coming to naught. In assessing the strains of commitment, it is perfectly admissible to imagine how ordinary men and women would regard the basic structure of their society, given the best social and psychological knowledge available. We are considering real people now, not idealized parties to an original position—in other words, people with the full range of imperfections, emotions, mutual attachments, and so forth. The social psychology of ordinary human beings may argue in favor of some principles over others.

From this point of view, let us consider a mixed conception of social justice that replaces the difference principle with a utility-maximizing principle, or libertarianism, which replaces the difference principle with a system of natural liberty. (Note that, although Rawls's argument in § 29 will be effective against either, it is not presented as such. Officially, mixed conceptions are not considered until chapter 5, and libertarianism is not explicitly considered at all.) Referring back to Figure 3.7 for a moment, imagine that the numbers in these columns represent bundles of social and economic goods under different configurations of the basic structure—different economic systems, say.

If we suppose that happiness is generally a linear function of shares of goods, other things being equal, then it follows that utilitarianism would opt for basic structure IV, in which the sum total happiness is maximized. Notice, however, that some will fare rather poorly under this system. What we must consider is whether those who fare badly will remain committed to utilitarianism regardless. "Allegiance to the social system may demand that some should forgo advantages for the sake of the greater good," says Rawls.

Against utilitarianism /

Thus the scheme will not be stable unless those who must make sacrifices strongly identify with interests broader than their own. But this is not easy to bring about. . . . The principles of justice apply to the basic structure of the social system and to the determination of life prospects. What the principle of utility asks is precisely a sacrifice of these prospects. We are to accept the greater advantages of others as a sufficient reason for lower expectations over the whole course of our life. This is surely an extreme demand. In fact, when society is conceived as a system of cooperation designed to advance the good of its members, it seems quite incredible that some citizens should be expected, on the basis of political principles, to accept lower prospects of life for the sake of others. (177–178; 155 Rev.)

It seems odd to expect some people to accept lower prospects of life for the sake of others, from the initial conception of the system

Crudely put, utilitarianism will tell the least advantaged members of society something like this: We're sorry things did not work out for you, but you should at least take comfort in the fact that your unhappiness has made it possible for others to be much happier, and their happiness outweighs your unhappiness! Given what we know about the social psychology of ordinary human beings, this will likely be a hard sell. Keep in mind that we are talking here about the least advantaged in terms of overall life prospects as determined by the lottery for natural talent and the basic structure of society. It is comparatively easy, perhaps, to turn aside complaints from those who have made poor life choices, and are unhappy as a result. The real difficulty is to answer complaints from those who started from behind even *before* they made any life choices. How can such involuntary disadvantages be justified? The least advantaged are unlikely

Real difficulty is people born into shitty situation, bad luck of the draw – under utilitarian view

to be moved by utilitarian arguments. Thus the strains of commitment, if we select utilitarianism in the original position, will be very high.

Things will not be much easier if we adopt the libertarian conception of social justice. Though Rawls does not develop this thought, it is has been clear to many readers that similar considerations would apply. Libertarians might also opt for basic structure IV in Figure 3.7—not because it happens to maximize the sum total happiness, but rather because a pure capitalist society best approximates the system of natural liberty ideal (see Section 3.4.2). Again, however, we must justify to the least advantaged members of society any involuntary disadvantages they will face. In a libertarian society, the least advantaged would in effect be told that they should take comfort in the fact that their diminished life prospects are a necessary consequence of permitting others, more fortunate than themselves, to reap the maximum personal returns on their native talents and other structural opportunities within a system of natural liberty. This will probably be an equally hard sell. The strains of commitment for libertarianism will be just as high as those for utilitarianism.

A clever opponent of justice as fairness, however, might seem to have a response to the strains of commitment challenge. Why not brainwash people? For example, suppose it turns out that the most effective way to maximize the sum total happiness is to introduce the two principles of justice as fairness as a useful fiction. Thus, everyone in society is told that they have inviolable basic rights and that they should aim to maximize the prospects of the least advantaged. They will believe that justice as fairness is the official conception of social justice for their society, but in fact, it has only been introduced as a device for realizing utilitarianism. Similarly, we might imagine (though Rawls does not) some more sinister forms of propaganda: we might adopt utilitarian principles and reduce the strains of commitment by inventing some story about how sacrificing the interests of the least advantaged is necessary for the evolutionary advancement of the human species; or we might adopt libertarian principles and reduce the strains of commitment by inventing some story about God-given natural rights which must be respected at any cost. Rawls, fortunately, is prepared for such tricks: "we must not lose sight of the publicity condition," he reminds us.

[margin annotation: Critique of libertarianism using involuntary least advantage.]

The parties to the original position are charged with selecting principles that will serve as the public conception of justice for their society. If no one knows that utilitarianism is the true justification for the basic structure, for example, then utilitarianism is not the true public conception of justice. The public conception is the one actually used in that society to settle disputes and guide public policy. "If, for whatever reasons, the public recognition" of some conception of social justice would generate excessive strains of commitment, then "there is no way around this drawback. It is an unavoidable cost" of selecting that conception in the original position, and thus a serious argument against it (181; 158 Rev.). People deserve to know the real reason the basic structure of their society is the way that it is.

Justice as fairness with the difference principle faces no such difficulties with the strains of commitment. While it is true that, under the basic structure recommended by the difference principle, there will certainly be inequalities in the distribution of social and economic goods, the difference principle will have ensured that these inequalities have worked to everyone's advantage—and in particular, to the benefit of the least advantaged members of society. Thus from Group E's point of view in Figure 3.7, basic structure III grants them the best overall life prospects they can expect. In adopting the difference principle, the parties to the original position effectively agree to regard society as a system of cooperation based on the value of reciprocity. "by arranging inequalities for reciprocal advantage and by abstaining from the exploitation of the contingencies of nature and social circumstance . . . , persons express their respect for one another in the very constitution of their society." Put another way, justice as fairness manifests our "desire to treat one another not as means only but as ends in themselves" (179; 156 Rev.). This is, of course, Kant's Formula of Humanity. Later, Rawls will be even more explicit in connecting his theory with the moral philosophy of Kant.

This completes the second main phase of Rawls's argument for justice as fairness. Much, of course, remains to be done. For starters, there has been no explicit pairwise comparison made between justice as fairness and perfectionism; this is postponed until the end of chapter 5. More significantly, perhaps, although

Rawls has presented arguments for each of the two principles of justice as fairness considered separately, he has gestured only briefly towards a justification of their strict lexical ordering. Roughly, he suggests that the parties to the original position will rationally want to preserve opportunities for reflecting on and revising their fundamental aims and commitments once the veil of ignorance has been lifted (131 Rev.). It follows that only when circumstances "do not allow the effective establishment of these rights," would the parties "concede their limitation," and even then "only to the extent that" such limitations "are necessary to prepare the way for a free society" in the long run (152; 132 Rev., with some changes).[12] The real argument for the lexical ordering, however, is left until much later.[13] These details not withstanding, by far the most important and most influential aspect of *A Theory of Justice* remains the original position argument for the two principles we have reviewed here.

In the final section of the third chapter, Rawls returns to the topic of utilitarianism. These reflections are perhaps meant to recall to mind the earlier contrasts drawn between the two main competing conceptions of social justice (in §§ 5–6 and §§ 16–17). In an original position, as we have seen, strictly rational persons behind a veil of ignorance would reject utilitarianism and opt for justice as fairness instead. What does this tell us about the nature of the utilitarian conception? Among other things, it tells us that any plausibility it might have as a theory of social justice must derive from an entirely different source. It must rest on a very different view of society, for example. Rather than viewing society from the inside, as a fair system of mutual cooperation among citizens who regard one another as equals, utilitarianism views society from the outside, as would an impartial spectator. From such a perspective, it may seem there is no reason not to substitute the greater happiness of one person for the lesser happiness of another. Indeed, it may seem irrational not to do so. According to Rawls, however, "utilitarianism fails to take seriously the distinction between persons" (187; 163 Rev.). In other words, it fails to respect the fact that the life of each individual person has unique value for him or her, not to be casually sacrificed whenever it is outweighed by the interests of others. Many readers have found this to be a powerful expression of what is fundamentally wrong with utilitarianism.

109

Study questions
1. From the standpoint of the original position, would it be irrational to adopt utilitarianism instead of a principle of equal basic liberties?
2. Is there something wrong with a society that cannot justify its basic structure to the least advantaged, and so must resort to propaganda or useful fictions in order to reduce the strains of commitment?

3.9 THE INSTITUTIONS OF A JUST SOCIETY
(§§ 31–32, 34–39, 41–43)

The second part of *A Theory of Justice* is ostensibly about institutions. Its aim, according to Rawls, is "to illustrate the content of the principles of justice . . . by describing a basic structure that satisfies these principles and by examining the duties and obligations to which they give rise" (195; 171 Rev.). This, however, gives a somewhat misleading impression of what we actually find. Chapter 6, for example, is concerned with institutions only very indirectly (as we shall later see). Even more striking, the discussions in chapters 4 and 5 are very abstract and, in certain significant respects, highly indeterminate as to their recommendations. Nowhere do we find what we might, perhaps, have expected—namely, something like a detailed blueprint for designing or reforming the institutions of a real society such as the United States.

The explanation for this is that, initial appearances to the contrary, we have not left the original position. Although the most famous—and most important—aspect of the original position argument for justice as fairness appears in chapter 3 of *A Theory of Justice*, the argument is not actually completed in that chapter. Careful readers will begin to sense this when expressions such as "the only principle that the persons in the original position can acknowledge" (207; 181 Rev.), or "from the standpoint of the original position" (217; 191 Rev.), resurface in Chapter 4; any lingering doubts should be erased once Rawls begins to revise the principles of justice as fairness and introduce new priority rules in their specification around the middle of chapter 5. The remainder of that chapter is then devoted to completing (finally) the case for justice as fairness against its main competitors.

The intended role of Rawls's explicit discussion of institutions (primarily in chapter 4 and the first-third of chapter 5) can be roughly explained as follows. Recall that the parties to the original position are supposed to be strictly rational. Among other things, this means that we should assume they will take into due consideration whether the principles of social justice they select can realistically be implemented. They might reject, for example, principles that are entirely unworkable in practice, even if they are very appealing in theory. Now of course, still being in the original position, the parties cannot make determinations as to this or that specific public policy or institution, since the veil of ignorance obscures from view many particular facts about the circumstances of their society relevant to such determinations. The best they can do is consider various possible circumstances A, B, C, and so forth, and speculate how the implementation of the principles of justice they settle on would look if their society faced circumstances of type A, or circumstances of type B, and so on. Rawls even suggests a framework they might use in imagining this process of implementation— what he terms "the four-stage sequence" (more on this shortly). The fact that we are still imagining people in an original position, however, who do not know the particular social and historical circumstances of their society, explains the often abstract and indeterminate nature of the discussion. It also explains the ongoing process of revising the principles of justice as fairness. In an easily missed earlier passage, Rawls notes that his aim in part two will be to test the principles of justice as fairness by comparing "their consequences for institutions and . . . their implications for fundamental social policy" with "our considered judgments," and that this testing is itself a part of his argument for that conception (152; 132 Rev.). Until both parts of the argument are complete, we have not finally arrived at reflective equilibrium.

As mentioned above, Rawls envisions in § 31 a "four-stage sequence" for working out how a theory of social justice might be selected and implemented. The first stage is the original position itself: in this stage, people select basic principles that will serve as the public account of social justice for their society, and they make this selection from behind a veil of ignorance that excludes any knowledge of either their personal characteristics or the particular circumstances of their society. The second stage corresponds to a constitutional convention in which people design a system of government and constitutional law for their society, using the principles selected in the first stage as their guide. For Rawls this mostly entails implementing the first principle of justice as fairness—the equal basic liberties principle. In order to ease this implementation, we are to imagine the veil of ignorance has been partially lifted in the second stage: although the representatives at the constitutional convention are still not permitted to know any personal facts about themselves, they are now permitted to know the particular circumstances of their society (its level of economic development, its geography and natural resources, its culture and history, and so forth). While it is true that real constitutional conventions are not like this—the participants in real conventions of course know a great deal about themselves and the parties and interests they represent—nevertheless it is often not possible for even the cleverest of constitutional designers to foresee how choices regarding basic political forms will help or hinder particular interests in the long run. Thus the envisioned second stage is not so idealized as it might first appear.

Once a system of government and constitutional law has been settled on, we enter into the third stage, corresponding to the process of setting public policies and socioeconomic regulations. It is in this stage, according to Rawls, that the second principle of justice as fairness—fair equality of opportunity and the difference principle—would be implemented. As in the second stage, however, the participants in the process of legislation are supposed to be constrained by a partial veil of ignorance. When it comes to determining ordinary policies and regulations, as distinct from designing constitutions, this assumption is perhaps less realistic. Indeed, given that the information available in stages two and three is assumed to be the same, we may wonder what the point of distinguishing between them is at all. Put another way, since our aim in the second stage is to implement the first principle of justice as fairness through the instrument of constitutional law, why should the second principle not also be entrenched in the constitution of a just society? The explanation is that Rawls supposes "a division of labor" necessary for dealing "with different questions of social justice." In his view, it is relatively easy to implement basic rights and liberties in the form of categorical and unconditional laws such as "the legislature shall make no laws restricting the free exercise of religion," whereas implementing the difference principle, say, will be much more difficult and will probably require an ongoing process of experimentation and revision through complex public policy initiatives. Moreover, it is "often perfectly plain and evident when the equal liberties are violated," whereas by contrast, "this state of affairs is comparatively rare with social and economic policies regulated by the difference principle" (199; 174 Rev.). It follows, according to Rawls, that the second principle of justice cannot effectively be entrenched in constitutional law. Its implementation requires a separate stage of its own.

The fourth and last stage is the stage in which public agencies, the justice system, and ordinary citizens respect the institutions and carry out the policies adopted in the previous two stages. In this stage, of course, there is no veil of ignorance: everyone knows exactly who they are and what the circumstances of in particular situation happen to be. Rawls will discuss this fourth stage later (in chapter 6).

To sum up, we see that Rawls divides the general problem of institutional design—the application of justice as fairness to the design of major political, social, and economic institutions and practices—into two main parts, corresponding to the middle two stages of the four-stage sequence: the first relates to the form of a society's government and its constitution, the second to its social and economic policies. Before turning to consider his remarks on each, it is perhaps worth reiterating that concrete recommendations will not often be forthcoming. This is because the process of implementation is still being imagined from the point of view of persons in the original position, who do not themselves have access to the specific information necessary for resolving the relevant problems. In other words, we are considering what persons behind a full veil of ignorance *imagine will happen* once the veil begins to lift, since this may influence their selection of basic principles in the original position itself. In a sense, we never actually leave the original position in *A Theory of Justice*, and for many readers, this is bound to be frustrating. On the positive side, however, it means that Rawls can largely remain agnostic as to the sort of society we happen to live in; his conclusions are not parochially tied to the specific circumstances of late-twentieth century American society, for example.

Let us turn first, then, to questions of constitutional design—that is, the design of the fundamental political and legal institutions of a just society. Broadly speaking, according to Rawls, constitutional design should be guided by two considerations. The first, and most important, is that the fundamental political and legal institutions should reflect the equal basic liberties guaranteed unconditionally by the first principle of justice as fairness. The second, and subsidiary, consideration is that, among the set of feasible constitutional configurations satisfying the equal basic liberties principle, we should select the one we can expect to be most reliable in generating public policies promoting the other aims of justice as fairness—namely, of securing fair equality of opportunity and of maximizing the prospects of the least advantaged (221; 194 Rev.). With respect to the first consideration, Rawls further notes that configurations of political and legal institutions can fail to reflect the equal basic liberties principle in two ways: either by granting some people more basic liberties than others, or by granting insufficient basic liberties to people in general (203–4; 178 Rev.). With these initial considerations in mind, he goes on to discuss some particular examples.

The first group of examples, discussed in §§ 34–35, concerns the limits of toleration, and is presumably intended to illustrate the operation of the first principle of justice as fairness with respect to our liberties of conscience and expression. Among other things, Rawls addresses the perennial debates as to whether such liberties can legitimately be regulated on behalf of public order, and whether they should extend even to intolerant persons or groups who would not grant them to others (he answers yes to both). The second group of examples, discussed in §§ 36–37, concerns the design of governmental institutions, and thus illustrates the operation of the first principle with respect to political rights and liberties. Here Rawls defends the public financing of political campaigns, for example, and the institution of judicial review. He also observes that justice as fairness "does not define an ideal of citizenship; nor does it lay down a duty requiring all to take an active part in political affairs" (227; 200 Rev.). The third and last group of examples, discussed in § 38, concerns the design of the legal system, thus illustrating the operation of the first principle with respect to what are sometimes called our legal or due process rights. These include such requirements as that the law must be performable, that it must treat like cases alike, and that judges must be independent and impartial. Roughly speaking, Rawls argues, the first principle of justice as fairness, when applied to a legal system, generates the requirements traditionally associated with the ideal of the rule of law. These sections are each interesting in their own right, but are also relatively straightforward, and so do not require further explication here.

Moving on to the second general problem of institutional design, which relates to the implementation of the second principle of justice as fairness through social and economic policies and regulations, we find a much briefer discussion in the opening sections of chapter 5 (§§ 41–43). This is no doubt due to Rawls's belief that such questions are considerably more complex, and thus less amenable to the contributions of a philosopher. Remarkably, he does not even try to resolve the important basic question of which economic system justice as fairness actually recommends. The idea is perhaps to delegate to expert economists and social scientists the task of determining which configuration of institutions and policies would, under given cultural and historical conditions, best maximize the prospects of the least advantaged. What Rawls offers instead are some very general remarks intended to suggest how such investigations ought to proceed; in offering his remarks, he relies heavily on the work of other notable political economists.[14]

Let us say that some societies, broadly speaking, are characterized by mostly public ownership of the means of production. Among these, some centrally plan all or most aspects of economic activity—how much of which goods will be produced, what their prices will be, and so on, whereas others delegate such determinations to markets. Rawls refers to these first two systems of political economy as the "command" system and the "socialist" system, respectively. Both are contrasted with societies in which the means of production are mostly privately owned. Among these, some aim to be pure free market economies, whereas others restrain the effects of markets through public provisions for basic needs, redistributive taxation, monopoly regulation, and so on. Rawls refers to these second two systems of political economy as the "capitalist" system and the "property-owning democratic" system, respectively. Now command systems are ruled out, he claims, on the basis of the first principle of justice as fairness: complete central planning of the economy will necessarily restrict our basic liberties as to choice of occupation, residence, and so forth. So too are pure capitalist systems, on the basis of the second principle: they make no provisions for improving the conditions of the least advantaged members of society. In principle, however, Rawls believes that either a liberal democratic socialist society or a property-owning democracy might be compatible with justice as fairness. In a given society, facing its own particular historical and other circumstances, which of these two will in fact tend to maximize the prospects of the least advantaged is a question for the professional economists and social scientists to work out.

In later work, we should note, Rawls further refines his views on political economy. Specifically, he felt compelled to introduce between the property-owning democratic system and the pure capitalist system a fifth option, which he refers to as "welfare-state capitalism" (2001: 139–140). Roughly speaking, this would be a generally capitalist society in which public spending ensured that no member of society fell below some defined threshold level of well-being. Essentially, on this system, the wealthy would boost the position of the least advantaged through side payments. This is not what Rawls had in mind, and thus he takes some pains to distinguish such a system from a genuine property-owning democracy in which the least advantaged are not simply bought off, so to speak, but actually embraced and incorporated within a system of fair cooperation. His concern was with the possibility that under welfare-state capitalism, the least advantaged—while materially provided for up to a certain threshold—would form a permanent underclass, and thus not enjoy a genuine fair equality of opportunity. A property-owning democracy would be a society in which policies and regulations are designed specifically so as to ensure this does not happen.

Before moving on to our next topic, it is interesting to observe that in § 39 Rawls briefly considers the question of whether it will be possible for any society, regardless of its circumstances, to fully realize justice as fairness. Specifically, will it always be possible to grant equal basic liberties to all unconditionally? (The difference principle is perhaps less demanding, in the sense that it only directs us to do the best we can for the least advantaged; its mandates might be satisfied even if we can only do a very little.) By lexically ordering the two principles of justice, "the parties are choosing a conception of justice suitable for favorable conditions and assuming that a just society can in due course be achieved," says Rawls (245). Under less favorable conditions, however, this "due course" might extend over many generations. Basically, the two lexically ordered principles are supposed to represent an ideal to be striven for over the long run. The parties to the original position imagine what sort of society they would *want* to live in, once it has become fully developed. They then select justice as fairness as the principles appropriate for *that* society. In the meantime, Rawls admits, "it may be necessary to forgo" a strict implementation of the principle of equal basic liberties when this is required to "transform a less fortunate society" into one where all the basic "liberties can be fully enjoyed" (247; 217 Rev.).[15] Any such departures from the priority of liberty, however, "must be acceptable to those with the lesser liberty" (250; 220 Rev.).

Study questions

1. Should the implementation of the difference principle be left entirely to ordinary political processes, or should it—like the equal basic liberties principle—be supported by explicit constitutional provisions?
2. Might a welfare-state capitalist society satisfy the demands of the difference principle and the principle of fair equality of opportunity?

3.10 COMPLETING THE ARGUMENT (§§ 40, 44–50)

Having more or less concluded his discussion of how the basic structure in a just society would reflect the two principles of justice, Rawls finally begins to wrap up his argument for justice as fairness in the middle of chapter 5. In order to do this, however, he must address some crucial remaining ambiguities in the formulation of the second principle. The more important of these ambiguities concerns how we are to weigh the interests of future generations against those of the present generation; below we will consider Rawls's answer to this complex problem in some detail.

First, however, we may briefly note another ambiguity, which concerns how we are to reconcile the two clauses of the second principle—that is, the principle of fair equality of opportunity and the difference principle. Often, of course, the two clauses will be perfectly compatible. This is because restrictions on the fair equality of opportunity usually detract from the overall economic productivity of society, and thus reduce the pool of resources available for enhancing the prospects of the least advantaged. This will not always be the case, however. Recall that fair equality of opportunity requires that we ensure the overall life prospects of persons in the different groups of society are not significantly influenced by factors such as their racial, cultural, or economic circumstances. Now in some societies, achieving this might only be possible through massive subsidies for education, through affirmative action policies, and so forth. These sorts of policies and institutions will presumably carry substantial social costs; indeed, they might cost so much as to effectively reduce the absolute well-being of the least advantaged. In situations like these, it will be difficult to satisfy the fair equality of opportunity principle and the difference principle at the same time. Which principle should then have priority?

Rawls considers this question in § 46, and answers that the fair equality of opportunity should have lexical priority over the difference principle. Put another way, we can imagine that fair equality of opportunity operates as a side-constraint on the difference principle: policies and institutions should be designed to maximize the prospects of the least advantaged so far as this is consistent with maintaining a fair equality of opportunity.[16] If this seems unduly demanding, it is perhaps worth reminding ourselves that Rawls does not suppose perfect equality of opportunity is realistically obtainable (since we are not prepared to do away with the family as a social institution); satisfying the relevant side-constraint will thus apparently only require achieving some threshold level of fair equality of opportunity. Fortunately, "following the difference principle," in Rawls' view, "reduces the urgency to achieve perfect equality of opportunity" (301; 265 Rev.). As in the case of the priority of equal basic liberties,

Rawls recognizes that it may be impossible under less-than-favorable conditions to fully realize even a modest threshold of fair equality of opportunity; in such cases, we should strive to "enhance the opportunities of those with the lesser opportunity" first (303; 266 Rev.).

Unfortunately, an argument demonstrating that strictly rational persons in an original position behind a veil of ignorance would actually agree on this lexical ordering of the two clauses seems to be missing. Certainly, it does not appear where we would expect, in § 46. Elsewhere, Rawls vaguely suggests that the priority of fair equality of opportunity is somehow connected with the importance of self-respect: individuals excluded from significant opportunities are "debarred from experiencing the realization of self which comes from a skillful and devoted exercise of social duties"; since the social bases of self-respect are regarded as a primary good in the original position, such individuals "would be deprived of one of the main forms of human good" (84; 73 Rev.). It has been complained, however, that this is hardly sufficient to establish the required priority. Strictly rational persons in an original position might perfectly well recognize the value of self-respect, and aim to secure its bases when they can, but also decide that absolute levels of economic well-being simply matter to them more (Pogge 2007: 120–133). This may be an unresolved gap in Rawls's argument.

3.10.1 Intergenerational justice

Let us turn now to the difficult problem of intergenerational justice. Suppose we set out to implement the difference principle, which directs us to organize the basic structure of society so as to maximize the prospects of the least advantaged (subject to the fair equality of opportunity constraint). Initially, it may seem that this imposes a very heavy burden on society, one that cannot possibly be sustained in the long run. For example, in providing a generous social minimum, we may starve the economy of resources that could otherwise be invested in research and development. A society that aims to satisfy the difference principle might then begin to lag further and further behind other, less generous, societies, until the very programs designed to help the least advantaged are no longer economically sustainable. Thus we help the least advantaged of the present generation only to the detriment of the least advantaged in future generations.

According to Rawls, we should not interpret the difference principle so as to require shortsighted policies like these. Rather, he argues (in § 45) that we should regard the least advantaged members of future generations as deserving a moral consideration equal with that of the least advantaged members of our present generation. On the utilitarian view of things, the equal moral worth of all human beings is assumed as an axiom. Just as the happiness of a peasant should count the same as the happiness of a king, and the happiness of a woman should count the same as the happiness of a man, so too the happiness of a person who will live in the future should count the same as the happiness of a person alive today. It makes no difference *when* a person happens to live, on this view. But justice as fairness rejects the utilitarian view of things, and so it must establish the equal moral worth of different generations in some other way. Naturally, it does so through the device of the original position. Just as we do not know what our role in society happens to be, so too the veil of ignorance does not permit us to know what stage of development our society has reached—that is, the particular generation to which we belong. If we do not know *when* we happen to live, we will naturally be equally concerned with the well-being of every generation.

Rawls supposes that this concern would be reflected in the adoption of what he terms the "just savings principle," which (much like the principle of fair equality of opportunity) operates as a side-constraint on the difference principle. In other words, each generation is required by the second principle of justice as fairness to maximize the prospects of its own least advantaged only after it has first put aside the required savings for future generations.[17] "This savings may take various forms," he notes, "from net investment in machinery and other means of production to investment in learning and education" (285; 252 Rev.). With the advantage of hindsight, of course, this framing of the problem of intergenerational justice may seem a bit quaint, but then again Rawls was writing before the environmental conservation movement had really become a major force in western societies. It is now easy to see that the problem Rawls has raised is really much more general. There are a myriad of ways in which the policies, institutions, and practices of the present generation can significantly influence the well-being of future generations for better or worse, manifest in such issues as global climate change, the maintenance of biodiversity, nonrenewable resource consumption, and so on. Fortunately, Rawls's discussion can easily be applied to these broader topics as well. To keep things simple, however, let us continue with Rawls's language here. The central question, addressed in § 44, is as follows: what level of savings is required, as a matter of social justice, from each generation?

To answer this question properly, on Rawls's view, we must consider it from the perspective of a strictly rational person in an original position behind a veil of ignorance. How might things look from this perspective? Suppose we imagined that each person in the original position did not know to which generation he or she individually belonged. In this case, it would only be rational for him or her to agree on some sort of just savings principle, so as to ensure that the first generation does not consume everything it can, leaving the following generations in destitute poverty. After all, why would you gamble on the small chance that you will turn out to be a member of that fortunate first generation? Supposing some such agreement were made in the original position, the only difficulty would then lie in ensuring that the various members of each generation held up their end of the bargain once the veil of ignorance had been lifted. Here, perhaps, we might rely on and encourage the natural tendency of human beings to care about the well-being of their descendants.

Curiously, however, the argument does not take this turn. Rawls explicitly declines to imagine the parties to the original position as each individually representing different generations. Instead, he insists that the parties to the original position are all members of the *same* generation, though the veil of ignorance does not permit them to know *which* generation this happens to be. Given the consequences of this move, as we shall see in a moment, it is surprising that Rawls offers so little justification for it. In § 44, he refers us back to an earlier passage in part one, which merely states that the alternative would "stretch fantasy too far," at which point the device of the original position "would cease to be a natural guide to intuition" (139; at Rev. 120, the former clause is changed to "would lack a clear sense"). This is hardly satisfactory, but a number of deep concerns, unmentioned by Rawls, might motivate such an assumption. One difficulty is that policies and institutions can affect not only the well-being of future generations, but also their *composition*—how many people there will be, for example. It is thus not clear how membership in the original position should be determined. Should it include only people who will necessarily live, regardless of the policies we adopt? Or should it include all the people who might possibly live? These sorts of mind-bending questions are rendered irrelevant in Rawls's framing of the problem.

Unfortunately, assuming that the parties to the original position are all members of the same generation raises different problems. What would such parties, if strictly rational, agree to? Granted, they do not know which generation theirs happens to be; nevertheless, since they do know they are all members of the same generation, they also know that whatever generations turn out to have preceded them have already saved whatever they have saved (or not). The pool of resources presently available has thus already been fixed, and it cannot be altered by anything decided on in the original position. Likewise, the parties to the original position have nothing to hope or fear from future generations, which are effectively powerless to help or hurt them. Given these parameters, what would strictly rational persons—where rationality has explicitly been defined as always preferring more primary goods to less—decide to do? It seems we must concede that they would decide to consume as much as they can for themselves: they would impose on themselves no obligation to save for the benefit of future generations. Once the veil of ignorance has been lifted, of course, actual human beings might naturally be disposed to care about the well-being of their descendants, and this might move them to make charitable provisions for the latter. Such provisions would apparently not be required as a matter of social justice, however.

This is not the conclusion Rawls wants to draw. How then does he avoid it? He simply stipulates, as was noted in earlier discussions of the model, that the parties to the original position themselves (much like actual human beings) are supposed to care for the well-being of their descendants. Since "it is assumed that a generation cares for its immediate descendents," he writes, "a just savings principle . . . would be acknowledged" in the original position (288; passage omitted in Rev.). It has rightly been pointed out that this is really cheating. The whole point of the original position device is to derive, so far as we are able, moral conclusions from nonmoral premises. It is thus deeply dissatisfying to find that we can extract from the parties in the original position a concern for future generations only by imputing to those parties that same concern (Barry 1977: 501– 506). Perhaps sensing the initial version of the argument would not satisfy, Rawls introduces a secondary consideration in the revised edition of *A Theory of Justice*. Basically, he imposes an extra formal constraint on the parties, namely, that whatever principles they adopt in the original position, they must "wish that all preceding generations to have followed the very same principles" (111 Rev.; cf., 255 Rev.).

Now it is unclear what the basis for this extra formal constraint is supposed to be. Even less than the previously discussed formal constraints of generality and universality (see Section 3.7), it cannot plausibly be derived from the distinctive role that principles of social justice are supposed to serve; nor can it be reconstructed as the mere upshot of deliberations behind a veil of ignorance, given our assumption that the parties are all members of the same generation. Even brushing aside these concerns, however, the requirement will fail for the same reason Kant's expression of the categorical imperative in the Formula of Universal Law failed. Here we must observe that the new formal requirement cannot mean that the parties must select a single savings rate applicable to all generations; this possibility is excluded by the fact that the just savings principle Rawls believes they will indeed adopt (see below) is a variable one, assigning different rates to different generations. But then, knowing they are all members of a single generation (and not some earlier one), it seems open to the parties in the original position to simply wish that all generations follow the principle 'every generation prior to the current one save as much as they can, while all the others consume as much as they choose'.[18] In short, it must be said that Rawls leaves the puzzle of intergenerational justice very much unsolved.

Leaving the difficulties aside, what is the just savings principle that Rawls believes the parties in the original position will adopt?

Roughly speaking, he imagines they will draw up a savings schedule that assigns to each possible generation a particular rate of savings. The rate will begin relatively low, so as to not overburden earlier generations. This compensates them, in effect, for having the misfortune of living in earlier, less prosperous, times. As the society becomes wealthier, the obligation of savings steadily increases, but not indefinitely; at some point, the society will achieve durable and fully just social institutions and practices. (From earlier remarks, we may infer that this basically means the society has become prosperous enough to fully implement both the equal basic liberties and a fair equality of opportunity, and indeed has done so.) At this point, an obligation to save above what is necessary to sustain that level of prosperity ceases. In other words, there is no obligation *as a matter of social justice* to make future generations more prosperous as such, though of course saving to that or others ends is always permissible, and might be supportable on other grounds (287–288; 255 Rev.). To reiterate what was said earlier, the just savings principle operates as a side-constraint on the difference principle. Each generation is supposed to maximize the prospects of its least advantaged, but only to the point that this is consistent with first setting aside the savings required of it by the schedule agreed to in the original position. Having done this, we have satisfied our obligations of justice to future generations.

3.10.2 The argument concluded

After presenting the final version of the two principles in § 46, with all their various special priority rules and side constraints, Rawls devotes the remainder of the fifth chapter of *A Theory of Justice* to finishing the argument for justice as fairness. He begins, curiously, with an extended reply to a set of objections that will probably not have occurred to many readers. To understand what is going on here, it may help to refer back to our earlier discussion (in Section 3.3) regarding the method of reflective equilibrium. Employing this method, we are supposed to begin with our considered judgments about a concept—social justice, say—and then try to construct a theory that explains them in something like a systematic manner. Since we are unlikely to capture all of our initial intuitions with a single theory, however, we must eventually decide which of these to hold on to and which to drop. In constructing his theory of justice as fairness, for example, Rawls began with the initial intuitions that justice is more important than efficiency, that religious intolerance and racial discrimination are unjust, and so on. After a long process of exposition and revision, we have now finally arrived at a statement of the theory we are reasonably happy with. As expected, it neatly captures these initial intuitions in a compelling and systematic manner.

Might there be other plausible intuitions about social justice, however, that the theory of justice as fairness fails to capture? Indeed there might, and in §§ 47–48 Rawls finally gets around to mentioning some of them. Consider for example the "tendency of common sense to suppose that income and wealth, and the good things in life generally, should be distributed according to moral desert" (310; 273 Rev.). Our initial intuition might be that it is unjust when a distribution of goods does not reflect the relative moral worth of persons: more virtuous persons *deserve* more. Now it should be clear that justice as fairness does not and cannot fully capture such intuitions. This is because, as Rawls reminds us, "it contains a large element of pure procedural justice" (304; 267 Rev.). In other words, provided that the basic structure of society is just according to the two principles, it is up to individuals to decide how to live out their lives, according to their own particular conceptions of the good. There can be no guarantee that the shares of goods people end up with, playing by the rules of the game, so to speak, will reflect any independent measure of their moral virtue. Moreover, no such principle will ever be imposed in a just society, because the parties to an original position behind a veil of ignorance would never agree to such a principle. How could they, given that the veil of ignorance prevents them from knowing their particular moral values? Without such information, how can they know which measure of moral desert they should adopt? In place of the notion of moral desert, justice as fairness substitutes the idea of legitimate expectations. If a person plays by the rules of a just society, she is legitimately entitled to whatever share of goods she secures through her participation in the system defined by those rules. Entitlements, in other words, are merely an upshot of the system, not criteria for evaluating it.

Is it an objection to justice as fairness that it cannot account for all our initial intuitions with respect to social justice? It is not. As we saw in our discussion of intuitionism, our common sense intuitions often conflict. There is no way to resolve such conflicts except by developing a more systematic theory to adjudicate between them, and this is precisely what justice as fairness does. It will serve no purpose to complain that, in such adjudications, some of our conflicting intuitions must give way to others. The only alternative is to build a better theory.

After setting aside such objections, Rawls returns to the task of slogging through pairwise comparisons between justice as fairness and its competitors on the list of alternatives (see Section 3.8). Next up to the plate are mixed conceptions. But these were already addressed in the strains of commitment argument, as Rawls clearly recognized only in his later writings. As a result, the actual discussion in § 49 is thoroughly anticlimactic. It merely runs through a few *additional* objections that might be levied against such theories, and here it must be admitted that the objections hardly seem decisive considered in themselves— that is, apart from the compelling strains of commitment argument canvassed earlier. For the most part, these objections relate to the practical difficulties we would face in attempting to implement a utilitarian principle in place of the difference principle. Moral and political philosophers have long been aware of such practical objections, however, and Rawls's discussion adds little to what has been ably said by others.

Moving on to the next section (§ 50), Rawls finally gets around to addressing perfectionist theories. The argument is again anticlimactic. This is because it should be obvious that the argument from basic liberties (deployed against unmixed utilitarianism theories) will be equally decisive against perfectionism. Recall that perfectionist theories start with a conception of the good as some specific form of human excellence—artistic or cultural achievement, say, or religious piety. They then go on to define justice as the honoring or promoting of this good. Now it is simply incredible to believe that the parties to an original position would ever agree to such a doctrine: to "acknowledge such a standard would be, in effect, to accept a principle that might lead to a lesser religious or other liberty if not to a loss of freedom altogether" (327; 288 Rev.). Given that the veil of ignorance hides from the parties all knowledge of their particular moral and other commitments, they clearly would not consent to such restrictions.

This brings chapter 5, and indeed the original position argument for justice as fairness, to a close. It is hardly a rousing conclusion, however. Far better in this regard is the concluding section to chapter 4 (§ 40), which explicitly reflects on the deep connections between justice as fairness and Kant's moral philosophy. In considering these reflections, we bring the discussion full circle, in a sense, returning to the initial motivation behind *A Theory of Justice*. Recall that Rawls's overriding aim was to develop a theory of social justice that might serve as a viable alternative to utilitarianism. What he realized was that nascent in the social contract tradition and in Kant's moral philosophy were the core insights on which such an alternative might be built.

There are many relevant points of connection between Rawls's theory of social justice and Kant's moral philosophy, but one that is especially important is the idea that (according to Kant) in acting on a categorical imperative, we are in a sense acting autonomously—that is, we are acting on the rule we would give ourselves. Morality, as Rawls puts it, is an "object of rational choice" (251; 221 Rev.). This thought is expressed, for example, in Kant's Formula of Universal Law, which directs us to act according to that maxim which we would will to be the maxim for everyone. Now we earlier observed that there is apparently a serious loophole in the Formula of Universal Law. It seems perfectly open to a prejudiced person to will that everyone follow the maxim "always discriminate against minorities (but not others)," since, let us assume, she knows she is not herself in a minority group. Fortunately, this "defect is made good," Rawls observes, "by the conception of the original position" (255; 224 Rev.). The veil of ignorance prevents the parties to an original position from knowing their particular characteristics. This effectively compels them to universalize their desires in the right way: not knowing whether they are themselves in the majority or the minority, they are compelled to adopt principles that are fair to everyone.

Having thus closed the loophole, Rawls can build on the underlying insight that autonomy means acting from the rule we would give ourselves. The same thought is expressed in Rawls's theory as the idea that a just society is one in which the basic structure reflects those principles of social justice the citizens would choose for themselves under fair conditions. Such a society would constitute, so far as this is realistically possible, a voluntary scheme of mutual cooperation. Consulted under fair conditions (i.e., in an original position), the citizens themselves would never accept the principles of utilitarianism, which might often entail sacrificing the interests of some merely for the benefit of others. Such principles would violate Kant's Formula of Humanity, which directs us to never treat other people merely as a means. Instead, according to Rawls, they would adopt the principles of justice as fairness.

Study questions
1. How might an original position argument succeed in addressing the problem of intergenerational justice?
2. Has Rawls succeeded in demonstrating that the parties to the original position would select justice as fairness over all its competitors on the list of alternatives?

3.11 JUSTICE AND THE INDIVIDUAL (§§ 18–19, 51–59)

Although the second part of *A Theory of Justice* is titled "Institutions," the final chapter of part two (chapter 6) does not seem directly concerned with institutions at all. On the contrary, it discusses the duties and obligations of individuals, insofar as these relate to justice. This represents something of a detour from the main program of Rawls's book, which is focused on the problem of social justice—that is, the problem of determining which political and social institutions and practices would be most just. Why does this detour appear in the part of *A Theory of Justice* devoted to institutions?

Rawls does not really get around to clearly explaining the connection between the two topics until well into the chapter. It is best illustrated, perhaps, by an example of special interest to Rawls—civil disobedience. Recall that when Rawls began writing *A Theory of Justice*, the civil rights movement was achieving some of its greatest victories, and when he was finishing the book, protests against the Vietnam War were gripping the nation. The issue of civil disobedience was thus very much a live concern for Americans in general, and also for Rawls personally (given that he opposed the war, and that he was in a position to affect the draft deferment status of his students at Harvard). To what extent are we obligated as a matter of justice to conform to the demands imposed on us by the institutions and policies of our society? To what extent does justice demand that we disobey institutions and policies when they are manifestly unjust? These are important questions and, at the time Rawls was writing, unavoidable ones. It thus makes sense to attempt addressing them right after completing a discussion of how the principles of social justice and the institutions and policies of a just society relate to one another.

Characteristically, Rawls approaches the relevant issues in a dispassionate manner, through the lens of ideal theory. Suppose the parties to an original position have initially formulated a conception of justice roughly like justice as fairness. Their next job, as we have seen, is to work out what sorts of basic social and political institutions would best reflect the principles of that conception, and the "four-stage sequence" suggests a procedure for doing this. In the second and third stages of the sequence, the principles of justice as fairness are applied to the design of political institutions and social policies, respectively. Once reasonably just institutions and policies have been put in place, however, it is up to public officials and citizens to implement those institutions and policies. This is the fourth stage of the four-stage sequence. In the fourth stage, individuals will need additional principles to guide their personal conduct. What are the appropriate principles? Very roughly, we might say, people have some sort of obligation or duty to respect institutions and policies insofar as they are just—that is, insofar as they conform to the two principles of justice as fairness—but not otherwise. This, of course, leaves the door open to civil disobedience in cases where institutions or policies are not just. Before turning to that topic, however, there are some complications we must address.

These complications concern the *source* of individuals' duties and obligations. Here it is necessary to observe that one particularly obvious route to such a source is not available to Rawls. On the traditional social contract doctrine, our obligation to obey political authority derives from our expressed or implied consent to the terms of the social contract. In other words, we (the people) agree to obey, provided they (the public officials) respect our rights, and vice versa. The social contract is thus supposed to be binding for the same reason that ordinary contracts are binding—because we have a moral obligation to observe promises we have made in good faith. This moral obligation is the source of our duty to obey. This route is not available to Rawls, however, for the simple reason that the original position he envisions is strictly hypothetical. No one is obligated to perform a business contract, say, he or she might have made hypothetically. We are only bound to observe the agreements we have *actually made* (Dworkin 1973: 16–19). Thus, the source of our individual obligations and duties with respect to justice must be found elsewhere. According to Rawls, they can be found in the same way that the principles of social justice are generally: through the device of the original position (this argument appears in §§ 18–19 and §§ 51–52). After settling on principles of social justice for institutions, the parties are imagined to consider a range of possible principles for individual conduct. Among the various principles they would agree on, Rawls believes, two are of special importance: what he describes as an obligation of fairness and a natural duty of justice.[19]

The obligation of fairness is roughly the obligation a person has "to do his part as defined by the rules of an institution," provided, first, that "the institution is just," and second, that the person "has voluntarily accepted the benefits of the arrangement or taken advantage of the opportunities it offers to further one's interests" (111–112; 96 Rev.). This obligation is what might be called an agent-relative obligation. In other words, it is binding on particular individuals only insofar as they are related to others in specific ways. Suppose that Andrea has promised to give $100 to Bob in repayment for a favor. First notice that she might not lie under this obligation if she had actually declined Bob's favor, but he performed it anyway; also notice that, having accepted the favor voluntarily, Andrea's obligation to Bob is not performed by her giving $100 to Carla instead. Our obligation to keep our promises is thus agent-relative in the sense that it obtains only between those particular human agents who are related through actual promises. The obligation of fairness, according to Rawls, is similarly agent-relative. If some group has adopted a set of institutions for their cooperative benefit, and if I voluntarily engage in cooperation with the members of that group, taking advantage of the fact that they all observe the rules their institutions impose, then it is only fair that I do my part, in turn, to observe and maintain those same institutional rules. Within the framework of his theory of justice as fairness, this will generally mean observing and maintaining the just basic political and social institutions set up during the middle two stages of the four-stage sequence.

The obligation of fairness will not be sufficient for all purposes, however. This is for two reasons. The first reason, emphasized by Rawls, is that it will clearly apply only to those persons who have actively and voluntarily taken advantage of the opportunities provided by the basic structure. It might not apply to individuals who have never endorsed the basic structure of their society, or perhaps to individuals who could make an argument that they personally have been disadvantaged by its present arrangement. The obligation of fairness thus applies most strongly to "those who assume public office, say, or those who, being better situated, have advanced their aims within the system" (116; 100 Rev.). Its force might be much weaker, or even negligible, with others. The second and perhaps more important reason, which Rawls does not explicitly mention, is that the obligation of fairness provides individuals little guidance in those situations where just institutions are simply absent. It does not seem to be enough to say that we have no justice obligations or duties in such cases.

It is for these reasons that Rawls introduces the natural duty of justice. Unlike the obligation of fairness, the natural duty of justice is not agent-relative—it is rather what might be called a universal duty. Suppose Andrea encounters someone who has slipped in a fountain, hit his head, and fallen unconscious. Without her aid, he will drown, but with her aid, he can be saved easily. Clearly, Andrea has a duty to help him. Notice that her duty here does not depend on her having some special relationship with this person in particular, nor on her having previously volunteered to accept responsibility for helping others in general. The duty to rescue is a universal duty. The natural duty of justice, according to Rawls, is similar. It is our universal duty "to support and to comply with just institutions that exist," and also "to further just arrangements not yet established, at least when this can be done without too much cost to ourselves" (115; 99 Rev.). According to this duty, individuals should endeavor to set up just institutions when they do not exist, and generally comply with them when they do. Again, within the framework of his theory, just institutions here refer to the basic political and social institutions set up during the middle two stages of the four-stage sequence.

In §§ 51–52, Rawls tries to show that these two principles for individuals, among some others, would indeed be agreed to in an original position from behind a veil of ignorance. There is little difficulty in seeing why this should be so. What is more difficult is seeing how their agreement can solve our initial problem— namely, of discovering the source of individual obligations and duties as they relate to justice. Suppose we grant that social just-ice is what people would (hypothetically) agree to in an original position. What then constrains individuals to further social justice, that is, the content of that agreement? The natural duty of justice. So what is the natural duty of justice? Apparently, it is the principle for individuals that people would (hypothetically) agree to in an original position. What then constraints individuals to observe *this* duty, that is, the content of their (second) agree-ment on how to best further the content of their (first) agreement? The argument seems headed towards an infinite regress, and Rawls unfortunately does not provide us an obvious escape.

Perhaps the most charitable solution is to emphasize the word "natural" in Rawls's expression "the natural duty of justice." The thought here is that there are some moral obligations or duties we have that are simply primitive—that is, obligations or duties that cannot themselves be derived from some sort of prior voluntary agreement, hypothetical or otherwise. Admittedly, there does seem to be something a bit incongruous about a theory of justice based largely on consent that cannot carry the logic of consent all the way through, but perhaps this is unavoidable. To get a consent-based argument off the ground, it may simply be necessary to posit some initial, *prima facie* moral commitments that do not themselves derive from consent. If so, we might say that the natural duty of justice is precisely this primitive moral commitment. We might thus read Rawls's argument as an attempt to show that the parties to an original position would *recognize* that they are already bound by something like a natural duty of justice. Their job in the original position is then to determine the just institutions and practices to which this natural duty refers—the institutions and practices they are supposed to create, respect, and comply with.

Suppose we go along with Rawls, and accept that something like the natural duty of justice and the obligation of fairness generally constrain individuals to comply with just institutions and policies. This brings us back to the question posed at the opening of this section: How far do these duties and obligations extend? With respect to the obligation of fairness, he notes that "it is not possible to be bound to unjust institutions, or at least to institutions which exceed the limits of tolerable injustice" (112; 96 Rev.). Presumably, the same applies with respect to the natural duty of justice. It follows that individuals clearly have a right to engage in at least nonviolent methods of disobedience to unjust institutions and policies. Indeed, in societies that are seriously unjust, "militant action and other kinds of resistance are surely justified" according to Rawls (368; 323 Rev.). But these cases are less interesting philosophically. More interesting is the case of a reasonably just society with only a few unjust institutions or policies; and most interesting of all is the limit case of a fully just society, in which the two principles of justice as fairness have been implemented as carefully and as thoroughly as it is possible to do under real-world conditions. Would civil disobedience have a role even in such nearly or fully just societies? Surprisingly, perhaps, the answer is yes.

Rawls explains the reasons for this answer in §§ 53–54. In brief, this issue comes down to the inherent limitations on our ability to design political and legal institutions. Recall that back in the second stage of the four-stage sequence, we were supposed to imagine a constitutional convention in which basic political and legal institutions are designed according to two main considerations: first, that the fundamental political and legal institutions should reflect the equal basic liberties guaranteed by the first principle of justice as fairness; and second, that among the set of feasible constitutional configurations satisfying the equal basic liberties principle, we should select the one we can expect to be most reliable in generating public policies promoting the other aims of justice as fairness—namely, of securing fair equality of opportunity and of maximizing the prospects of the least advantaged. Now clearly, the second consideration represents an example of what Rawls refers to as "imperfect procedural justice" (see our discussion in Section 3.4.4). Our aim in adopting a procedure—the procedure of majority rule voting, for example—is to maximize the likelihood that just, rather than unjust, policies will be produced. But unfortunately, "there is no feasible political process which guarantees that the laws enacted in accordance with it will be just. In political affairs," Rawls observes, "perfect procedural justice cannot be achieved" (353; 311 Rev.). It follows that even in a fully just society, and certainly in one somewhat less than fully just, the political system will generate at least a few unjust laws and policies.

Should we disobey such unjust laws and policies? In general, according to Rawls, we should not. The natural duty of justice and the obligation of fairness constrain us to respect the (imperfect) outcomes of a political system that is largely just according to the two principles of justice as fairness. There are exceptions, however, in which Rawls believes that civil disobedience is both permissible and appropriate. Civil disobedience is defined as "a public, nonviolent, conscientious yet political act contrary to law usually done with the aim of bring about a change in the law of policies of a government" (364; 320 Rev.). Here Rawls is clearly regarding the American civil rights movement in the 1950s and early 1960s as his model. Under what circumstances is this sort of disobedience permissible and appropriate? According to Rawls, there are three conditions (372–375; 326–329 Rev.): the first is that the injustice in question be substantial and clear; the second is that attempts to achieve reform through ordinary political processes have been made in good faith and failed; and the third is that too many groups do not all engage in civil disobedience at the same time, undermining the rule of law. What sorts of injustice count as being "substantial and clear?" Only serious infringements of the equal basic liberties principle and blatant violations of the fair equality of opportunity principle. Injustices arising under the difference principle, apparently, will not ever be sufficiently clear or substantial in his view.[20]

Having thus defended the resort to civil disobedience, at least in certain circumstances, Rawls goes on (in § 59) to argue that it can be a stabilizing—not destabilizing—factor in a just society. Civil disobedience, he suggests, "can be understood as a way of addressing the sense of justice of the community, an invocation of the recognized principles of cooperation among equals" (385; 337 Rev.). By invoking the principles of justice, the minority engaged in civil disobedience will engage the majority in reflection on their commitment to those principles. Additionally, Rawls points out, the possibility of civil disobedience acts as a disincentive to adopting unjust laws and policies in the first place. Thus we find that civil disobedience has an important role even in a society that is mostly or fully just according to the principles of justice as fairness.

As an addendum to this discussion, it is worth briefly noting that Rawls also considers the problem of conscientious refusal, primarily through contrast with civil disobedience. He defines as conscientious refusal as "noncompliance with a more or less direct legal injunction or administrative order" addressed to a particular individual (368; 323 Rev.). At the time he was writing, the especially prominent instance was of course people's refusal to comply with the Vietnam War draft, though historically there have been many other cases. Since conscientious refusal does not have a specific role in the theory of justice as fairness, but is rather an issue of balancing our individual duties and obligations with respect to social justice against our other personal moral commitments, Rawls goes into less detail here. His comments are mainly interesting insofar as he briefly sketches an account of global justice from which we might derive principles of just war, by way of providing a nonreligious example of where our other moral commitments might come from. Sometime later, in his book *The Law of Peoples* (1999b), Rawls develops this account of global justice in greater detail.

Study questions

1. To what extent is it an objection to a consent-based theory of social justice that it must rely on some moral duties and obligations that do not themselves derive from consent?
2. Is it appropriate to limit the use of civil disobedience to clear violations of the equal basic liberties principle and the fair equality of opportunity principle?

3.12 THE SEARCH FOR STABILITY (§§ 60–87)

Here we arrive at the third and final part of *A Theory of Justice*. Although this part runs well over a 150 pages, our discussion will be limited to a single section. The reason for this has already been explained. Rawls's aim in part three is to give an account of stability—in other words, to show that in a well-ordered society, whose basic structure reflects the two principles of justice as fairness, the citizens will tend to endorse and support social justice. Later Rawls came to view his account of stability as deeply flawed, however, and indeed internally inconsistent with the theory as a whole. Accordingly, he developed a new account of stability, based on the idea of what he termed an "overlapping consensus" (see esp. Rawls 1985, 1993). Since this new account officially superceded the old, it is customary to give scant attention to the third part of *A Theory of Justice*. In light of these developments, the aim of this section will be to briefly explain the account of stability as it appeared in part three, while also conveying some sense of why Rawls later came to regard that account as unsatisfactory.[21]

In *A Theory of Justice*, Rawls understands an account of stability as essentially a solution to what he terms the "problem of congruence." Suppose that we have established a well-ordered society whose basic structure reflects the two principles of justice as fairness. In order for that society to be stable, on Rawls's view, it must make sense for each individual citizen to adopt something like the natural duty of justice as a central part of his or her personal conception of the good. So doing, the citizens would not only strive to observe and maintain just institutions and policies in their actions, but they would further shape their own personal goals and aims in such a manner as to reflect a commitment to social justice. They might, for example, formulate only those sorts of personal life plans that are consistent with regarding others as free and equal citizens. No one would set out to become a slave master, or to promote religious intolerance. In Rawls's language, a person who adopts something like the natural duty of justice as a part of his or her personal conception of the good affirms justice "as regulative of their plan of life" (567; 497 Rev.). Well-ordered societies in which all, or nearly all, citizens have incorporated social justice into their personal conceptions of the good will be highly stable for fairly obvious reasons: since none of the citizens in such a society have good reasons for resisting or undermining its institutions and policies, the social system as a whole will constitute an especially robust equilibrium. The problem of congruence, then, is the problem of showing that it is indeed possible for the particular conception of justice as fairness to find a comfortable home within people's personal conceptions of the good—our theory of social justice and our theory of the good for a person must somehow be shown "congruent" with one another.

Rawls attempts to solve the congruence problem in three stages, which roughly correspond to the three chapters of part three. In the first stage (chapter 7), he attempts to articulate a very general or "thin" theory of the good—what he terms "goodness as rationality." The need for a thin theory arises because, as we have repeatedly observed, people do not all share a single conception of the good. These differing conceptions of the good arise from the obvious fact that in large and diverse societies, different people adopt different plans of life: some aim to become talented doctors, others to become faithful Christians, others to become champions for the environment, and so on. What is good for each individual person will inevitably depend to some extent on what their particular plan of life happens to be. For the purposes of addressing the problem of congruence, however, it is necessary to have a general theory that captures what all these particular conceptions have in common. What they have in common, according to Rawls, is rationality. Briefly, rational conceptions of the good must satisfy two conditions. First, they must possess a certain sort of internal coherence. For example, while it might be irrational to set out to become rich by going to seminary school, it might not be irrational to set out to become a good Christian by going to seminary school: the latter plan has an internal coherence the former seems to lack. Second, they must also be able to withstand some sensible degree of deliberative reflection. In other words, a conception of the good would be irrational if its plausibility depended on misinformation, or on a failure to consider how well suited it was to the particular talents and abilities of the person in question. The thin theory of goodness as rationality is thus simply the view that it is always better for a person to base their particular conception of the good on a rational life plan.

In the second stage of his discussion (chapter 8), Rawls tries to show that in a well-ordered society, governed by the principles of justice as fairness, people will usually tend to develop what he describes as a "sense of justice"—roughly, a psychological disposition to care about social justice to some degree. When a person has an effective sense of justice, she will include among the various goals or aims constituting her particular plan of life the specific goal or aim of furthering social justice. Although Rawls does not use this language exactly, we might think of the sense of justice as a desire to do what the natural duty of justice requires us to do. In order to show that a sense of justice on the part of the citizens will tend to emerge in societies governed by the principles of justice as fairness, Rawls relies on a number of assumptions drawn from basic social psychology. Although the details of this story are complex, the gist of it is that he regards it as a "deep psychological fact" that human beings are moved, at least to some degree, by a sort of reciprocity instinct. That is, we have a tendency to "answer in kind," injury for injury, and benefit for benefit (494; 433 Rev.). Growing up in a society organized as a fair system of mutual cooperation, he believes, most people will tend to develop the sense that they ought to each contribute their own fair share to the system that has benefited them. Ideally, this feeling will eventually mature into an effective sense of justice. Though plausible, this is of course an empirical claim that requires evidentiary support from the social sciences. For the sake of argument, however, let us suppose it is more or less true.

This brings to the third and final stage (chapter 9) of the discussion. In order to understand what is going on in this third stage, we must observe that an effective sense of justice is not necessarily sufficient to Rawls's purposes. It is not enough that citizens merely *have* a desire to further justice if that desire is not strong enough to actually *regulate* their life plans. In order to guarantee the stability of a well-ordered society, the citizens' sense of justice must be strong enough to actually override any contrary desires or inclinations that might operate to undermine that stability. To further complicate things, Rawls insists that the sense of justice must be strong in the right way. He does not want to achieve stability merely through a program of indoctrination that effectively turns citizens into justice-loving automatons. The stability in question must be the right sort of stability. For Rawls, this basically means demonstrating that it is *rational* for people to incorporate a sense of justice into their respective conceptions of the good—rational both in the sense that the sense of justice coheres with their other particular goals and aims, and also in the sense that its inclusion will withstand deliberative reflection. If we can demonstrate this, then we will have shown that the theory of justice as fairness is congruent with the thin theory of goodness as rationality. The demonstration appearing in chapter 9 has roughly two sides. On the one side, Rawls attempts to show that in a society governed by the two principles of justice as fairness, many of the usual sorts of destabilizing desires and inclinations would be greatly mitigated. For example, there would be no rational basis for envy on the part of the least advantaged in a society that sincerely strives to implement the difference principle. If he is right about this, our sense of justice will have less psychological resistance to overcome. On the other side, Rawls attempts to show that it is actually rational for us to embrace a system of fair mutual cooperation governed by the principles of justice as fairness, regardless of our particular conception of the good. Very roughly, this is because, first, it is only though our participation in such a system that we can fully realize our diverse talents and abilities; and second, in affirming that system, we are expressing our autonomy in the Kantian sense of living according to the rules we have given ourselves.

This, in outline, is how the account of stability appeared in part three of *A Theory of Justice*. Now what prompted Rawls to change his mind? The difficulty was caused by his growing appreciation of what he later termed "reasonable pluralism." We have already observed that in large diverse societies, people will naturally tend to formulate different conceptions of the good based on different plans of life. Nevertheless, what Rawls envisioned was a well-ordered society in which everyone affirmed the same conception of justice as fairness on the same grounds. Each particular citizen's conception of the good was supposed to fit as a sort of interchangeable module within what Rawls would later call a "comprehensive doctrine." The comprehensive doctrine in question was a sort of Kantian vision of a fully voluntaristic society—a society in which, through our affirmation of justice as fairness, we each express both our own personal autonomy, and also our respect for others as valuable and distinct ends unto themselves. But herein lies the contradiction. It is precisely in liberal societies respecting the first principle of justice as fairness that people will naturally tend to formulate not only diverse conceptions of the good, but also diverse comprehensive doctrines as such. Of course this would not be a problem (philosophically, at any rate) if the Kantian comprehensive doctrine were simply true, and the others false. In that case, we could simply dismiss the deeper sort of diversity as the result of ignorance. Unfortunately, this is not the case. We cannot establish with certainty that the Kantian comprehensive doctrine is true, and the others false. Even after we dismiss those comprehensive doctrines that clearly rest on false premises or errors in reasoning, there will remain some range of comprehensive doctrines that all seem reasonable. This is the fact of reasonable pluralism.

The fact of reasonable pluralism requires an entirely new account of stability. Without going into the details, what Rawls proposes in his later writings is that we adopt a more modest stance towards justice as fairness. Instead of viewing justice as fairness as part and parcel of a specific Kantian comprehensive doctrine, we begin with the assumption that the latter is only one of several equally reasonable comprehensive doctrines. Much as diverse conceptions of the good can fit as modules within a particular comprehensive doctrine, so too can diverse conceptions of social justice. But while a society benefits from having an internal diversity of conceptions of the good, it must have a broadly shared public conception of social justice in order to resolve disputes concerning the configuration of its basic structure. The trick is then to find a single conception of social justice that can fit as a module within all the reasonable comprehensive doctrines. Rawls strives in his later writings to show that justice as fairness can do this—that it can serve as the focus of what he calls an "overlapping consensus" of reasonable comprehensive doctrines (see esp. Rawls 1985, 1993). This forces a number of changes to justice as fairness. Among other things, justice as fairness must be shorn of any residual dependencies on the particularly Kantian comprehensive doctrine so that it can become "freestanding," as Rawls puts it. A freestanding conception of social justice does not rely on the truth of any one comprehensive doctrine in particular, and so can fit more easily as a module within many different ones. In order to render his conception freestanding, Rawls modifies his account of primary goods and his argument for the lexical ordering of the two principles of justice, for example. A detailed discussion of these changes, however, would take us well beyond the scope of this Reader's Guide.

A Theory of Justice does not have a proper conclusion. The final section of chapter 9 (§ 87) more or less serves in that role. There Rawls reviews the nature of the argument for his conception of justice as fairness. This argument, as we saw in the discussion of reflective equilibrium (see Section 3.3), is neither foundationalistic nor naturalistic. A foundationalistic argument would start with a small set of first principles regarded as self-evidently true, and attempt to derive a theory of justice on that basis. A naturalistic argument would attempt to relate moral propositions to nonmoral ones, and then proceed to search for empirical evidence that the latter are indeed true. By contrast, the reflective equilibrium method strives for a broader sort of coherence among our considered moral and nonmoral views. The argument of *A Theory of Justice* is thus supposed to be that justice as fairness, better than utilitarianism or other competing conceptions of social justice, fits with and accounts for the values and beliefs to which we are already most strongly committed. These stronger commitments include, for example, our belief in the wrongness of slavery and our conviction that justice is the first virtue of social institutions. In his rousing final paragraph, Rawls suggests that the device of the original position uniquely enables us to "bring together into one scheme all individual perspectives and arrive together at regulative principles that can be affirmed by everyone . . . , each from his own standpoint" (587; 514 Rev.). Only in this way, he believes, can we regard society from an impartial point of view, while at the same time respecting the uniqueness of each separate human life.

Study questions
1. To what extent, if any, does the argument in *A Theory of Justice* depend on a controversial Kantian conception of human autonomy?
2. Has Rawls succeeded in his main aim, providing a compelling and powerful alternative to utilitarianism?

CHAPTER 4

RECEPTION AND INFLUENCE

4.1 *A THEORY OF JUSTICE* AS A CLASSIC

Having been in print for less than 50 years, it is of course too early to assess the ultimate historical importance of *A Theory of Justice*. Nevertheless its influence as a work of political theory and philosophy, even in such a brief time, has been astounding. It is thus reasonably safe to predict that Rawls's book will come to be regarded as one of the very few, really great philosophical classics of the twentieth century.

This is not to suggest that all political theorists and philosophers now agree with Rawls, or that there is anything like a consensus on the merits of his conception of justice as fairness. Far from it, as we shall see. Regardless of how such debates turn out, however, and regardless of whether the specific conception of justice as fairness continues to command significant academic support, there are at least three respects in which Rawls's book so decisively transformed its field as to virtually guarantee its eventual status as a classic. The first is that it revived political (and to some extent moral) philosophy from its mid-twentieth century slide into relative obscurity. At the time Rawls began his work in the 1950s, political philosophy had become a moribund discipline. *A Theory of Justice* completely changed this state of affairs: it is now a widely respected field of study, with thousands of scholarly practitioners. The second is that it decisively ended utilitarianism's hegemony over moral and political philosophy. While utilitarianism certainly retains a serious and respected— if much diminished—following, it is no longer the only game in town. Not only are contractualist theories now considered a viable alternative, but in the wake of Rawls's initial success many new theories have also emerged.

The third transformation wrought by *A Theory of Justice* is considerably more subtle than the first two, though perhaps ultimately even more significant. It concerns the very conceptual framework within which political philosophy operates. Part of the reason that political philosophy had earlier gone into decline was that it had not kept pace with developments in the broader fields of philosophy and social science. These fields had made great forward strides with respect to their sophistication and rigor since the nineteenth century. In relative contrast, it became less and less clear what a good argument in political philosophy was supposed to look like, or indeed what it was even supposed to be about. *A Theory of Justice* changed all that. Here was a massive work, of manifest sophistication and rigor, addressed to clearly important problems in political philosophy. Initially, many people did not quite know what to make of it. The methods and techniques employed were so novel that many misunderstood just what Rawls was doing. (This is evident in some of the early book reviews by philosophers and social scientists, for example.) Its significance gradually sank in, however. Many of the basic ideas found in *A Theory of Justice*—ideas such as reflective equilibrium, basic structure, primary goods, procedural justice, fair reciprocity, and so on—have become standard parts of the repertoire of political philosophers: tools of the trade, so to speak. Even when they are attacking Rawls's specific views, indeed even when they are discussing something basically unrelated to Rawls, contemporary political theorists and philosophers, more often than not, speak in the language of Rawls.[1]

For these reasons, and perhaps more, *A Theory of Justice* is destined to become a philosophical classic, even if its particular conception of justice as fairness ceases to command a significant following. The remainder of this section will review in outline some of the more significant substantive debates surrounding *A Theory of Justice* since its publication. Of these, probably the most significant was the so-called liberal-communitarian debate of the 1980s.

4.2 THE LIBERAL-COMMUNITARIAN DEBATE

In order to set the stage for this debate, it is first helpful to have a sense of the direction political philosophy moved in the years immediately after Rawls's book was published in 1971. As we have seen in this Reader's Guide, the arguments presented in *A Theory of Justice* are extremely complex, and have many interrelated aspects. It is perhaps not surprising, then, that initially some aspects of the theory were emphasized in academic discussions at the expense of others.

Specifically, we might recall that in the original position argument, Rawls assumes the veil of ignorance will hide from the parties any knowledge of their particular conceptions of the good. The principles of justice emerging from the original position could thus be described as "neutral" in the sense that their derivation does not hinge on the truth or falsity of any one conception of the good in particular. This independence seems to give the principles of justice a sort of superiority over particular conceptions of the good. For example, while it seems wrong to press public policies supported merely by a controversial conception of the good that not all citizens share, public policies supported by a universal conception of the right (the purportedly neutral principles of social justice) seem more acceptable. This idea was often summed up in a slogan, derived from various passages in Rawls: "the priority of the right over the good."

Now in the years immediately following the publication of *A Theory of Justice*, many political theorists and philosophers began to strongly emphasize the idea expressed in this slogan. Three quite diverse examples illustrate this tendency. First we might first consider Robert Nozick's *Anarchy, State, and Utopia*, published in 1974. This work directly challenged Rawls's theory of justice as fairness from a broadly libertarian point of view. Nozick elevated individual rights against any sort of unwanted interference to the role of an absolute standard against which all other moral and political considerations were considered trivial. On his view, the state has no business involving itself in any sorts of collective projects at all: its only job is to enforce our individual rights. To the extent that citizens hold personal conceptions of the good, it is entirely up to them to try to realize those conceptions through their own activities in the private sphere, provided of course that they do not violate the rights of others in the process.

Two other books, written by legal scholars, similarly illustrate this tendency: one is Ronald Dworkin's *Taking Rights Seriously*, which was published in 1977; the other is Bruce Ackerman's *Social Justice in the Liberal State*, published in 1980. Interestingly, both these authors are liberal egalitarians like Rawls, and thus reject the harsher libertarian views expressed in Nozick's work. Nevertheless, both demonstrate the same tendency to emphasize the priority of the right over the good. Dworkin elevates the role of individual rights in political discourse, arguing that they should be understood as absolute "trumps" on public policies whose aims stem from controversial conceptions of the good.[2] Similarly, Ackerman argues that any arguments depending in any way on controversial conceptions of the good should be excluded from the political sphere: only strictly neutral arguments are admissible grounds for public policy.

As will be no surprise, there eventually developed a backlash against these views. What is somewhat surprising, however, is that the backlash did not take the form of rejecting these later ideas and returning to a more balanced reading of Rawls. Instead, the backlash took the form of a direct assault on Rawls himself. Perhaps this was because, despite their many differences, Rawls, Nozick, Dworkin, and Ackerman were all seen from the perspective of the early 1980s as sharing in the same distinctively liberal idea that conceptions of the right are neutral, and therefore universal and absolute, whereas conceptions of the good are controversial, and therefore parochial and subordinate. As the senior and most respected member in this group of liberal theorists, Rawls was naturally singled out by those who wanted to oppose its doctrines, whether he was really their most suitable target or not. It is perhaps also worth noting that what came to be called the "communitarian critique" of the 1980s corresponded roughly with the rise of mainstream conservative movements in British and American politics. Although this is not entirely a coincidence, it would be a mistake to assume that the communitarian critics were all political conservatives. Some were, but the most influential (including all those mentioned in the following discussion) generally were not; they simply disagreed with the particular turn that liberal political philosophy had taken in the later 1970s.

One of the most significant of the communitarians was another Harvard political philosopher, Michael Sandel. His most important work, *Liberalism and the Limits of Justice*, which appeared in 1982, levels a cumulative series of arguments against Rawls. The first is that, appearances to the contrary, the liberal conception of justice as fairness is not at all neutral towards diverse conceptions of the good. On the contrary, Sandel claims, the whole argument in *A Theory of Justice* crucially depends on a notion of the human good as a Kantian sort of autonomy to shape our own ends as we please. If Sandel is right about this, then the right cannot really be prior to the good, as had been claimed. Like it or not, we must start with a particular and perhaps controversial conception of good, and work out a conception of justice from there. In the second stage of his attack, Sandel examines the particular liberal conception of the good as Kantian autonomy, and finds it wanting. Drawing on the writings of others—most notably those of the Hegelian scholar Charles Taylor—Sandel tries to show that we are not really autonomous beings, unencumbered by values and commitments we did not choose for ourselves. Nor would we want to be. In a certain deep respect, on the communitarian view, it is precisely our involuntary attachments to friends, family, community, and so forth that define who we are as people and what we regard as most important in our lives. Third and finally, Sandel points out that if we nevertheless embrace the unappealing liberal conception of the good as Kantian autonomy, we will find in the end that it undermines, rather than supports, the very aims of justice as fairness. In particular, support for the difference principle crucially depends on our willingness to see ourselves as bound up with others in a fair system of mutual cooperation. The liberal conception of the good as Kantian autonomy, unfortunately, runs directly counter to this sense of mutual attachment: it promotes individualism, at the expense of community.

The communitarian critique of liberalism suggested several routes for further development or response. The most obvious route, perhaps, was to embrace the critique, and then try to work out what an alternative, more communitarian theory of justice might look like. This was more or less the route followed by another very influential communitarian, Michael Walzer. On his communitarian view of social justice, roughly speaking, we start with a particular conception of the good generally shared in a given human community. Then we go on to say that this "society is just if its substantive life is lived in a certain way—that is, in a way faithful to the shared understandings of the members" (Walzer 1983: 313). Principles of social justice appropriate for each community are thus derived from the particular shared values of that community. As such, they will of course vary from one place to another, and from one historical period to another. There are many possible objections to this line of reasoning, of course. For one thing, it seems to leave relatively little for the political philosopher or theorist to do, since the job of studying the shared values of this or that actual human community is perhaps best left to trained anthropologists. For another, it seems to entail an excessive degree of conservatism. This is because, deprived of the sure grounds provided by an independent conception of social justice standing apart from the shared values of a given community, it is difficult to see how the members of that community can criticize their own objectionable values and practices. Walzer, to his credit, admits as much, remarking that in communities embracing the values of a hierarchical caste system, for instance, the caste system must be regarded as just.[3]

An entirely different route was followed by Joseph Raz. In his book *The Morality of Freedom*, published in 1986, Raz more or less concedes the communitarian charge that liberalism depends on a particular and controversial conception of the human good as autonomy. On his view, however, what we should do is fully embrace this conception, develop its meaning, and argue that (contrary to the communitarian critics) it actually represents an attractive political ideal. Of course not all people actually accept the ideal of autonomy, historically or today, but that only goes to show that it is an ideal we should do more to promote. The upshot of this approach has been dubbed "liberal perfectionism" (or sometimes "ethical liberalism") in the literature. Recall that a perfectionist conception of social justice defines the good as the realization of some specific form of human excellence, and then characterizes the right as the promotion or honoring of that good. When Rawls was writing *A Theory of Justice*, the main examples of perfectionism he had in mind were various religious views, or the notion that human excellence resides in artistic and cultural achievement. Understandably, such views do not seem plausible when measured against justice as fairness. But once we define the good for human beings as the liberal ideal of autonomy itself, we have a much more interesting and attractive perfectionist conception, worthy of serious consideration.

Rawls himself, however, did not take either of these routes. In fact, we have already seen the route he did take in our brief discussion of how his views about the problem of stability changed after the publication of *A Theory of Justice* (see Section 3.12 in Chapter 3). It is interesting to consider the implications of these changes in light of the communitarian critique. As it happens, in the process of leveling his attack against Rawls, Sandel relied heavily on the earlier parts of *A Theory of Justice*, and especially on the original position model. This model, he argues, expresses a particular conception of human beings as autonomous and unencumbered beings with no prior attachments or commitments they have not chosen for themselves. As many commentators (and Rawls himself) later pointed out, however, this line of argument is seriously flawed. It rests on a fundamental misunderstanding of the role the original position model is supposed to play within the overall theory of justice as fairness. The model is merely a device of representation, not a metaphysical account of the human condition (Rawls 1993: 22–28).

Ironically, Sandel might have presented his argument with much greater effectiveness relying on part three of *A Theory of Justice*. This is because, in his attempt to solve the congruence problem in part three, Rawls does indeed rely at various points on a Kantian ideal of human autonomy. Indeed, he effectively admits as much when he later says that an "essential feature" of the account of stability appearing in *A Theory of Justice* is the assumption that in a well-ordered society, all the citizens endorse justice as fairness as part of a "comprehensive philosophical doctrine" (Rawls 1993: xvi). Sandel might then have argued that the liberal comprehensive doctrine in question was, for all intents and purposes, a controversial conception of the good.

Be that as it may, Rawls's revised account of stability supplies a response against even this more plausible version of the communitarian critique.[4] We are now supposed to envision a society in which justice as fairness serves as the focus of an overlapping consensus of diverse reasonable comprehensive doctrines. From one point of view, this might be seen as a tactical retreat on Rawls's part, insofar as he now admits that justice as fairness depends for its support on comprehensive doctrines. From another point of view, however, it represents a flanking move, insofar as justice as fairness does not depend on a single comprehensive doctrine being shared by all community members—and certainly not on their sharing the particular liberal-Kantian doctrine specifically. The new version of justice as fairness has proved considerably more robust in the face of communitarian-style criticism, and thus the liberal-communitarian debate more or less petered out with the publication of *Political Liberalism* in 1993.

4.3 FURTHER DEBATES AND CURRENT STANDING

The liberal-communitarian debate is certainly not the only controversy surrounding Rawls's work. This final section will briefly examine some of the other notable debates, before reflecting on the current standing of the work.

One group of debates arise from feminist discussions of Rawls. There are many different issues here, as for example whether the original position model can or should omit emotional reasoning, whether the assumption of mutually disinterested rationality improperly excludes romantic and other attachments, and so forth. In the interest of space, however, we may concentrate on what is probably the most important debate to arise from these feminist discussions—namely, the problem of the family as a social institution. In *A Theory of Justice*, apart from noting that the family is a part of the basic structure of society (7; 6 Rev.), and that we are probably not going to want to dispense with it (74; 64 Rev.), Rawls has comparatively little to say about how a full implementation of the principles of justice as fairness might affect its organization. This led to much speculation and debate. Sometimes it was assumed that he must hold a traditional view of the family, and his views were attacked on that basis. At other times, it was assumed that he intended to apply the two principles of justice directly to the internal organization of families—for example, insisting that parents apply the difference principle in distributing goods among their children. This led to a different set of complaints.

Rawls eventually tried to address these concerns in one section of a later paper titled "The Idea of Public Reason Revisited" (1997: 595–601). There he reaffirms both his view that the family is a part of the basic structure, and that it is something we are not going to be able to do without any time soon. However, he clarifies that the principles of justice as fairness should not be applied directly to the internal organization of families. He draws a parallel with the internal organization of churches. Let us suppose that, in a liberal society whose institutions and policies reflect the two principles of justice as fairness, churches are voluntary organizations. According to Rawls, the internal organization of a voluntary organization need not itself reflect the two principles; a particular church need not be internally democratic, for example. Nevertheless, voluntary organizations must respect the two principles of justice as a side constraint on whatever forms of internal organization they choose to adopt. They may not, for example, prohibit members from leaving the church, since this would violate the rights of free association guaranteed by the first principle of justice. Analogously, families must respect the two principles of justice as fairness: individuals must be free to form them and leave them as they choose, and no one can have his or her rights denied within them. Provided these limits are respected, however, the internal organization of families is beyond the appropriate scope of public concern.

Unfortunately, the parallel chosen by Rawls is not apt. This is because churches, like other voluntary organizations, are not themselves a part of the basic structure. Families are, however, as Rawls himself insists. They are a part of the basic structure because we effectively delegate to families the important job of social reproduction, and clearly the system for having and raising children significantly influences the eventual life prospects of those children in ways beyond their personal control or responsibility. From the point of view of children, families are not voluntary associations. The better parallel might be something like the internal organization of a criminal court. Clearly the criminal justice system is a part of the basic structure, but it is not the case that each and every part of the basic structure internally must reflect the two principles of justice as fairness. Criminal courts are not organized democratically, nor do they employ the difference principle in rendering their judgments. Rather, we should view the criminal justice system as one part of a complete institutional scheme, the whole of which is designed to best realize the two principles of justice. The social institution of the family is similar in this respect. While the internal organization of each family need not reflect the two principles of justice as fairness, as one part of a complex institutional scheme the institution of the family as a whole must carry out its distinctive role in that scheme in such a manner as to effectively realize the two principles of justice. Thus, if it turns out that delegating complete responsibility for education to parents will generate severe inequalities in the eventual prospects of children— inequalities that would violate the difference principle—then justice as fairness would require retracting or regulating that delegation.[5] This, at any rate, is the position that seems most consistent with his theory.

In addition to feminist discussions, there are numerous other debates surrounding themes first introduced by Rawls's *Theory of Justice*. For example, the idea of primary goods, together with the difference principle, has spawned an extensive and highly technical literature concerning distributive justice. Among other things, it is debated whether Rawls was right to argue that primary goods better capture what we should care about than happiness or welfare, or whether some other metric—levels of basic human functioning, say—is better still. It is also debated whether our focus should be on giving priority to the least advantaged, as Rawls argued, or rather on achieving equality, or on achieving a sufficient level of well-being for everyone. Still other debates revolve around questions such as whether justice as fairness should recognize multicultural rights, whether justice as fairness accords a sufficiently prominent place to democratic participation, whether we should regard the basic structure as the true subject of justice, and so on. Rather than consider each of these debates in detail, however, let us concentrate on one particularly contentious set of recent debates concerning the topic of global justice. Rawls only briefly considered such issues in *A Theory of Justice*. There he suggests that the original position procedure might efficaciously be employed in generating principles of global justice, much as it was employed to generate the two principles of social justice. He considers this thought only briefly, however, by way of supplying some possible non-religious grounds for conscientious refusal, and he gives little indication as to what principles such a procedure would generate, except to note that it would certainly include some of the more familiar principles of just war (377–379; 331–333 Rev.).

Thus an opening was left to others. Two particularly influential attempts to apply the reasoning behind justice as fairness to the problem of global justice are Charles Beitz's *Political Theory and International Relations*, published in 1979, and Thomas Pogge's *Realizing Rawls*, published in 1989. Both authors arrive at roughly similar conclusions. Start with the observation that, among the things that influence your life prospects in ways beyond your personal control are not only the institutions and practices constituting the basic structure of your own society, but also the particular circumstances of your society relative to others—for example, whether it is large or small, militarily powerful or weak, resource rich or poor, and so on. The obvious solution, it might seem, is to include people from all societies in the original position. Since the veil of ignorance hides from the participants any knowledge of their particular society, they will select principles for global justice that are fair to all people around the world. Specifically, Beitz and Pogge reason, the argument supporting the difference principle for one society must be equally strong in supporting a global difference principle across societies. The upshot seems to be that global justice demands fairly extensive redistribution from wealthy and advantaged societies to poor and disadvantaged societies. This redistribution, we can presume, would far exceed the paltry levels of foreign aid currently given.

In his later years, Rawls decided to address the problem of global justice himself, eventually publishing *The Law of Peoples* in 1999. Surprisingly, he did not endorse the conclusions that Beitz, Pogge, and others has arrived at. He rejected the idea of including people from all societies in the original position. Instead, he envisioned two different original positions. The first, corresponding to the original position laid out in *A Theory of Justice*, would take place separately in each society. Only after this would the well-ordered societies (roughly, those whose institutions in some measure respect the rights and interests of their members) send representatives to another, global original position. The representatives in this second original position would similarly be subject to a veil of ignorance, but they would of course know that they are representing only the interests of well-ordered societies, and not the interests of all societies, much less the interests of all individuals around the world. The upshot, according to Rawls, would be principles of global justice much more strongly committed to the autonomy of each society to confront its own problems in its own way, and much less strongly committed to global redistribution. These results may certainly be regarded as more realistic in light of the current state of international affairs, but nevertheless many of Rawls's supporters were seriously disappointed. They felt that Rawls had made unwarranted concessions to an unjust reality, and had failed to follow through the logic of his own ideas. Naturally, these remain hotly debated issues in the literature.

This last debate nicely illustrates the present standing of Rawls's work. Many political philosophers remain strongly committed to the principles introduced in *A Theory of Justice*, and even when they disagree with Rawls, as often as not the debates center around his views. So far, of course, we have discussed only the influence of *A Theory of Justice* in academic circles, which has been profound. What about its broader influence on society as a whole? Here we find a rather different picture. Unfortunately for Rawls, his work has had almost no effect on the direction of American or other societies. On the contrary, the broad historical trend since *A Theory of Justice* first appeared has generally moved away from his views—and this despite the fact that his book has sold many hundreds of thousands of copies, and has been translated into nearly 30 languages. In this respect, however, *A Theory of Justice* may experience a fate similar to many other great works of philosophy. It would be a grave mistake to judge the historical influence of works like John Locke's *Second Treatise of Government*, Adam Smith's *Wealth of Nations*, or Karl Marx's *Capital* on the basis of their first 50 years in print. Often it takes a century or more for philosophical works to begin to seriously shape the course of human events. From this standpoint, Rawls's *Theory of Justice* may yet have a still more remarkable future.

NOTES

CHAPTER 1

1 Further details regarding the biography of Rawls can be found in Pogge (2007) and Freeman (2007).

2 All references to *A Theory of Justice* will be given in this form, indicating the page or pages in the original (1971) edition of that work first, followed by the page or pages in the revised (1999a) edition.

CHAPTER 2

1 In Rawls (1955), this is presented as the most plausible interpretation of utilitarianism.

2 That it is not perfectly equivalent, however, will be observed later (see Section 3.8).

CHAPTER 3

1 Observe here that, as this example illustrates, utilitarians are not necessarily indifferent to the distribution of things *other* than happiness, since the distribution of things such as material goods might have an impact on the sum total happiness.

2 Note that a fourth possibility (combining the Difference Principle with Formal Equality of Opportunity) is designated the "Natural Aristocracy" interpretation, but not discussed in detail (74–75; 64–65 Rev.).

3 That is, assuming there are no transaction costs. Provided transaction costs are sufficiently low, however, the general point will more or less hold.

4 Or at any rate could be, to the extent that our disposition to cultivate our talents and abilities does not in turn partly depend "upon fortunate family and social circumstances," which apparently Rawls believes that it does (104; 89 Rev.). However, as we shall see, the main line of argument does not depend on this controversial claim.

5 More precisely, no rewards apart from the intrinsic pleasure one might derive from the cultivation of a talent. We have no reason to believe, however, that such intrinsic pleasures will generate a socially optimal schedule of incentives.

6 The discussion in this section might also be compared with that found in §§ 47–48, which further clarify and support the observations that follow.

7 Rawls outlines a theory of "goodness as rationality," from which these particular conclusions are supposed to derive, in §§ 61–64 of chapter 7 (see Section 3.12).

8 The role of this assumption in the argument for justice as fairness will be discussed in Section 3.8.1, and its role in the problem of intergenerational justice in Section 3.10.1.

9 Strictly speaking, of course, this conclusion only follows if—much like the first son of the deceased cattle rancher—he assumes that he will receive the *last* (and thus presumably worst) share. The veil of ignorance as described by Rawls does not actually warrant this assumption, since it prevents people in the original position from knowing only *which* share will be theirs. More on this shortly.

10 Observe that, to the extent that the following argument is sound, a person in the original position can be said to choose principles *as if* for "a society in which his enemy is to assign him his place" (152; 133 Rev.). This characterization of the relevant choice scenario, more prominent in earlier versions of his theory (e.g., Rawls 1958: 54), is downplayed in *A Theory of Justice*.

11 In the basic liberties argument, Rawls did not claim that people *are* risk averse, but rather that, under certain specific conditions, they *should* be; his claim was about the nature of rationality, not human psychology. The difficulty now is that the required conditions apparently do not apply when it comes to second principle.

12 Rawls expands on this somewhat elliptical concession at various points in the second part of *A Theory of Justice*: see Sections 3.9 and 3.10.

13 Specifically, it is left until § 82 in chapter 9. There he suggests that the parties to the original position will recognize that as the pressure to meet urgent material needs diminishes with economic and cultural development, the relative value of the basic liberties must eventually predominate. Alas, this observation, even if true, is nothing to the purpose (Hart 1973: 249–252). In later writings, Rawls attempted to fill in the missing argument for priority (see esp. Rawls 1993: 310–340).

14 In particular, his discussion is greatly indebted to Mill (1848) and Meade (1964).

15 Some have noticed that, in admitting this necessity, Rawls effectively implies the existence of a third principle of social justice, prior to the first principle of justice as fairness. This third principle requires societies to cross some threshold level of minimal economic development before attempting to fully implement equal basic liberties (see Barry 1973: 60–76; Pogge 1989: 134–148).

16 Expressing their relationship in this way may account for the curious fact that throughout *A Theory of Justice*, even right after explicitly emphasizing the priority of the latter, the second principle of justice is always written with the difference principle coming first; it also reveals this discussion as being of a piece with the discussion of intergenerational justice in §§ 44–45, which similarly introduces

a side-constraint on the difference principle. That said, in later writings, Rawls generally presents the two clauses in the order reflecting their actual priority.

17 Under certain economic environments, it might turn out that the just savings principle will not actually constrain the difference principle. This would happen if it turns out that the prospects of the least advantaged are in fact optimized by a configuration of economic institutions and policies which already generates the required savings, or more.

18 By way of parallel, imagine the parties to the original position knew there were two groups in society, the A's and the B's, and that they all happened to be members of the B group. If they were strictly rational, they might adopt a rule obligating all the A's to serve the interests of the B's. Notice that concealing the relative size of the two groups does nothing to change the result. Similarly, concealing which generation the parties belong to does nothing, so long as each knows she is not a member of one of the previous generations, however many of these there may turn out to have been.

19 Note that Rawls observes a terminological distinction between obligations (which he regards as arising out of voluntary acts) and duties (which he does not) that has not generally caught on in the literature. The discussion here will accordingly de-emphasize this distinction.

20 When considering these issues in an earlier section, however, Rawls characterized this condition somewhat differently. There he indicated that "the long run burden of injustice should be more or less evenly distributed over different groups in society, and the hardships of unjust policies should not weigh too heavily in any particular case." It follows that "the duty to comply is problematic for permanent minorities that have suffered from injustice for many years" (355; 312 Rev.). This might simply be an explication of the reason violations of the fair equality of opportunity principles count as clear and substantial, but it might also suggest conditions under which violations of the difference principle could rise to that level. Rawls does not clarify one way or the other.

21 For more detailed discussions, however, see Barry (1995) or Freeman (2007: esp. chapters 6–9).

CHAPTER 4

1 This is, of course, more generally true among Anglo-American political theorists and philosophers than among continental European ones, though his influence (with some delay) is spreading among the latter as well.

2 In later work, Dworkin (1990, 2000) has apparently moved away from this position and advanced a distinctive version of what is sometimes referred to as "ethical liberalism," a nonteleological

version of liberal perfectionism. Liberal perfectionism will be discussed briefly later in this section.

3 In some later works, however, he tries to show how social criticism is possible within a communitarian framework (see esp. Walzer 1993).

4 Here we should point out that Rawls himself insisted the changes in his view were the product of contradictions internal to the conception of justice as fairness itself, and in no way motivated by the communitarian critique. This claim is plausible in light of the fact that Rawls began to shift his views several years before Sandel's book appeared.

5 Within the constraints set by the first principle, of course, which protects individuals' freedom of association.

BIBLIOGRAPHY AND FURTHER READING

MAJOR WORKS BY RAWLS

Rawls, John. "Outline of a Decision Procedure for Ethics," (1951; reprinted in *Collected Papers* [ed. Samuel Freeman; Harvard University Press: Cambridge, MA, 1999]).

—— "Two Concepts of Rules," (1955; reprinted in *Collected Papers* [ed. Samuel Freeman; Harvard University Press: Cambridge, MA, 1999]).

—— "Justice as Fairness," (1958; reprinted in *Collected Papers* [ed. Samuel Freeman; Harvard University Press: Cambridge, MA, 1999]).

—— *A Theory of Justice* (Belknap Press: Cambridge, MA, 1971).

—— "Kantian Constructivism in Moral Theory," (1980; reprinted in *Collected Papers* [ed. Samuel Freeman; Harvard University Press: Cambridge, MA, 1999]).

—— "Social Unity and Primary Goods," (1982; reprinted in *Collected Papers* [ed. Samuel Freeman; Harvard University Press: Cambridge, MA, 1999]).

—— "Justice as Fairness: Political Not Metaphysical," (1985; reprinted in *Collected Papers* [ed. Samuel Freeman; Harvard University Press: Cambridge, MA, 1999]).

—— *Political Liberalism* (Columbia University Press: New York, 1993).

—— "The Idea of Public Reason Revisited," (1997; reprinted in *Collected Papers* [ed. Samuel Freeman; Harvard University Press: Cambridge, MA, 1999]).

—— *A Theory of Justice: Revised Edition* (Belknap Press: Cambridge, MA, 1999a).

—— *The Law of Peoples* (Harvard University Press: Cambridge, MA, 1999b).

—— *Justice as Fairness: A Restatement* (Belknap Press: Cambridge, MA, 2001).

WORKS ABOUT RAWLS

Barry, Brian. *The Liberal Theory of Justice* (Oxford University Press: Oxford, 1973).

—— "John Rawls and the Search for Stability," *Ethics* 105 (1995): 874–915.

Cohen, G. A. *Rescuing Justice and Equality* (Harvard University Press: Cambridge, MA, 2008).

Daniels, Norman (ed.), *Reading Rawls: Critical Studies on Rawls's "A Theory of Justice,"* (Stanford University Press: Stanford, CA, 1975).

Dworkin, Ronald. "The Original Position," (1973; reprinted in *Reading Rawls* [ed. Norman Daniels; Stanford University Press: Stanford, CA, 1975]).

Freeman, Samuel (ed.), *The Cambridge Companion to Rawls* (Cambridge University Press: Cambridge, 2003).
—— *Rawls* (Routledge: London, 2007).
Hart, H. L. A. "Rawls on Liberty and Its Priority," (1973; reprinted in *Reading Rawls* [ed. Norman Daniels; Stanford University Press: Stanford, CA, 1975]).
Kukathas, Chandran and Philip Pettit. *Rawls: A Theory of Justice and its Critics* (Stanford University Press: Stanford, CA, 1990).
Pogge, Thomas. *Realizing Rawls* (Cornell University Press: Ithica, NY, 1989).
—— *John Rawls: His Life and Theory of Justice* (Oxford University Press: Oxford, 2007).
Sandel, Michael J. *Liberalism and the Limits of Justice* (Cambridge University Press: Cambridge, 1982).
Wolff, Robert Paul. *Understanding Rawls* (Princeton University Press: Princeton, NJ, 1977).

OTHER CITED WORKS

Ackerman, Bruce A. *Social Justice and the Liberal State* (Yale University Press: New Haven, CT, 1980).
Barry, Brian. "Justice between Generations," (1977; reprinted in *Democracy, Power, and Justice: Essays in Political Theory*. Clarendon Press: Oxford, 1989).
Beitz, Charles R. *Political Theory and International Relations* (Princeton University Press: Princeton, NJ, 1979).
Dworkin, Ronald. *Taking Rights Seriously* (Harvard University Press: Cambridge, MA, 1977).
—— "Foundations of Liberal Equality," *The Tanner Lectures on Human Values* 11 (1990): 3–119.
—— *Sovereign Virtue: The Theory and Practice of Equality* (Harvard University Press: Cambridge, MA, 2000).
Kant, Immanuel. *Groundwork of the Metaphysics of Morals* (1785; ed. Mary Gregor; Cambridge University Press: Cambridge, 1997).
Meade, J. E. *Efficiency, Equality, and the Ownership of Property* (Allen and Unwin: London, 1964).
Mill, John Stuart. *Principles of Political Economy* (1848; ed. Jonathan Riley; Oxford University Press: Oxford, 1994).
Nozick, Robert. *Anarchy, State, and Utopia* (Basic Books: New York, 1974).
Raz, Jospeph. *Morality of Freedom* (Clarendon Press: Oxford, 1986).
Roemer, John E. *Theories of Distributive Justice* (Harvard University Press: Cambridge, MA, 1996).
Rousseau, Jean-Jacques. "On the Social Contract," in *The Basic Political Writings* (1762; trans. Donald A. Cress; Hackett Publishing: Indianapolis, IN, 1987).
Sen, Amartya. "Equality of What?," *The Tanner Lectures on Human Values* 1 (1980): 197–220.

Walzer, Michael. *Spheres of Justice: A Defense of Pluralism and Equality* (Basic Books: New York, 1983).

—— *Interpretation and Social Criticism* (Harvard University Press: Cambridge, MA, 1993).

INDEX

Ackerman, Bruce 145–6

basic liberties
  argument for justice as fairness
    from 97–102, 126–7
  and institutional
    design 114–15
  meaning of clarified 48–9
  as a primary good 67–9
  see also equal basic liberties
    principle
basic structure of society
  and considerations of
    publicity, efficiency, and
    stability 40–1
  defined 17–18, 24–5, 45
  and procedural justice 63–4
  as subject of justice 18–19,
    25–6, 45
Beitz, Charles 152–3
Bentham, Jeremy 4, 18, 34
Berlin, Isaiah 1

campaigns, public financing
  of 114
chain connection, defined 60
circumstances of justice *see*
  justice, circumstances of
civil disobedience 128–9, 133–5
civil rights movement,
  American 2, 128, 134
close-knit economic relations,
  defined 59
communitarian critique of
  liberalism 146–50
compliance, strict versus
  partial 26–7

comprehensive doctrines
  defined 139–40
  reasonable pluralism of 140–1,
    149–50
congruence, problem of 136–9
conscientious refusal 135

Declaration of Independence 8
Democratic Party, American 3
deontological theories,
  defined 33
  see also teleological theories
desert, moral 25–6, 52–5, 125
  see also justice, procedural
difference principle
  defined 56–9
  and equality of opportunity
    65, 118–19
  and the least advantaged
    57–8
  and solidarity 75
  see also justice as fairness,
    two principles of; second
    principle of justice as
    fairness
duty of justice, natural *see* justice,
  natural duty of
Dworkin, Ronald 145–6

efficiency, principle of 51–2,
  56–7
egoism, first-person versus
  general 91–2
Enlightenment Age 4
entitlements and legitimate
  expectations 125
  see also justice, procedural

equal basic liberties principle
  meaning of 47–9
  and pluralism 140
  see also justice as fairness, two
    principles of
equality of opportunity
  and the difference principle 65,
    118–19
  fair, defined 53–5
  formal, defined 51–3
  see also justice as fairness,
    second principle of

fairness, obligation of 130–1
  see also justice, natural
    duty of
family, social institution of 52–4,
  150–2
feminism 150
first principle of justice as
  fairness *see* equal basic
  liberties principle
formal constraints on
  conceptions of justice *see*
  justice, formal constraints on
Formula of Humanity *see* Kant,
  Immanuel
Formula of Universal Law *see*
  Kant, Immanuel
four-stage sequence 110–13, 129
functioning, basic human 69–70,
  152

good, conceptions of
  and diverse plans of life 68–9,
    71, 81, 137
  priority of right over 145–7
  and the sense of justice 138–9
  and the veil of ignorance 79,
    81–2, 100–1, 126–7
  see also comprehensive
    doctrines; teleological
    theories

Hampshire, Stuart 1
Hare, R. M. 1
Hart, H. L. A. 1, 48

individuals, principles of justice
  for 66, 128–33
  see also fairness, obligation of;
    justice, natural duty of
intergenerational justice *see*
  justice, intergenerational
intuitionism
  as an alternative to
    utilitarianism 5–6, 15
  defined 6, 36
  and the priority problem 36–7
  ruled out by formal constraints
    on conceptions of justice 91
  unreliability of intuitions
    and 37–8

Jefferson, Thomas 8
judicial review 114
just savings principle 120–1, 123–4
justice
  basic structure as the subject
    of 18–19, 25–6, 45
  circumstances of 80–1
  distributive 152
  formal constraints on
    conceptions of 88–91
  formal vs. substantive 45
  global 135, 152–4
  intergenerational 119–25
  mixed conceptions of 92–3,
    104–7, 126
  natural duty of 131–3, 136, 138
  and principles for individuals
    66, 128–33
  procedural 60–4, 73, 125, 134
  sense of 138–9
justice as fairness
  as an alternative to utilitarianism
    7, 20, 29, 44–5, 66–7

and basic liberties 47–9, 101–2
as a deontological theory 33
designed for a closed social
  system 26, 28
and economic institutions
  115–16
favorable conditions for the
  implementation of 116–17
fit with intuitions 49–50, 65
general conception of 47
informal argument for 94–6
and intergenerational justice
  121–4
main idea of 19–20, 27–30,
  75–6
and political institutions
  114–15
and primary goods 66–71
and the separateness of
  persons 71–2, 109
and solidarity 73–5
and strains of commitment 108
two principles of 28–9, 45–7,
  64–5

Kant, Immanuel
and doctrine of autonomy
  127–8, 139–41, 146–7, 149
and Formula of Humanity
  10–11, 108, 128
and Formula of Universal
  Law 11–12, 20, 123, 127
moral philosophy of 7, 9–12,
  20, 80, 108, 127–8

lexical priority
of basic liberties 46–7, 64–5,
  108–9
defined 46
of fair equality of
  opportunity 118–19
libertarianism 92, 104–7
Locke, John 7–8, 12, 19, 154

Marx, Karl 154
maximin choice method 98–101,
  103–4
McCarthyism 2
Mill, John Stuart 4, 18, 34–5
mixed conceptions of justice *see*
  justice, mixed conceptions of
multicultural rights 152
mutual disinterest *see* rationality,
  mutual disinterest and

New Deal 2
Nozick, Robert 62, 64, 145

original position
and the four-stage sequence
  110–11
hypothetical nature of 28, 76–8,
  130, 149
and intuitions 39, 39–41, 50,
  77–8
main idea of 27–9, 76, 86
presentation of alternatives
  in 87–8, 93–4
rationality of the parties
  in 82–5
representation of future
  generations in 85–6, 121–3
and traditional theory of the
  social contract 20, 27
and the veil of ignorance 78–82

perfectionism
defined 31, 92
liberal 148
rejected in the original
  position 126–7
and utilitarianism 34–5
plans of life *see* good,
  conceptions of
pluralism, reasonable *see*
  comprehensive doctrines,
  reasonable pluralism of

Pogge, Thomas 153
political economy, systems
  of 115–16
primary goods
  and basic human functioning
    69–70
  defined 67–9
  measurement of 70–1
  and rationality 68–9, 82–3
priority problem 36–7, 46
procedural justice *see* justice,
  procedural
publicity requirement 40–1, 90,
  107–8

rationality
  broader considerations of 40,
    84–5, 88–9, 111
  and mutual disinterest 83–4
  of the parties in the original
    position 39–42, 82–5,
    121–2
  and primary goods 68–9
  sense of justice and 139
  thin theory of 137–8
  and utilitarianism 31–2
Rawls, John
  biography of 1–2
  and writing of *A Theory of
    Justice* 2–3, 7, 12, 20–2
  and writing of *Law of
    Peoples* 135, 153–4
  and writing of *Political
    Liberalism* 13, 22, 140–1,
    149–50
Raz, Joseph 148
reflective equilibrium
  defined 42–4
  initial presentation of 12
  and the original position 50, 111
  and prior intuitions 124–6, 141
Rousseau, Jean-Jacques 7, 9, 28
rule of law 114–15

Sandel, Michael 146–7, 149
Sidgwick, Henry 35
second principle of justice as
  fairness
  democratic equality
    interpretation of 56–7, 62–4
  liberal equality interpretation
    of 53–5
  and procedural justice 61–4
  system of natural liberty
    interpretation of 51–3
  two parts of 49–50
  see also difference principle;
    equality of opportunity;
    justice as fairness, two
    principles of
sense of justice *see* justice,
  sense of
separateness of persons 71–2,
  109
Smith, Adam 154
social contract, traditional
  theory of 7–9, 19–20, 28,
  129–30
stability, problem of 22, 136–41,
  149–50
strains of commitment
  argument for justice as fairness
    from 103–9
  defined 105
system of cooperation, society
  as a 15–16, 24, 29–30, 75

Taylor, Charles 147
teleological theories, defined
  30–2, 92
  see also deontological theories
toleration, limits of 114

uncertainty, problem of choice
  under 98–101, 103
utilitarianism
  average vs. classical 96, 102

and basic liberties 33–4, 97–8,
100–2
defined 4–5, 30–6
difficulties with 5–6, 14–15
and the impartial spectator
71–2, 109
as indifferent to distribution
32–3
and intergenerational justice
120
procedural justice and 73
and reliance on intuitions 38–9
as a teleological theory 30–2, 92
as theory of social justice
12–13, 18–19, 26
and views concerning
happiness 34–6
utility monsters 32
utility theory *see* utilitarianism,
views concerning happiness
and

veil of ignorance
defined 20, 78–82
and formal constraints on
conceptions of justice 89–90
full vs. partial 111–13
and the original position 20,
27–9, 86
Vietnam War 2, 128
voluntaristic society, idea
of a 28, 76, 90, 127–8,
139–40

Walzer, Michael 147–8
welfare state 3, 116
welfarism 66–7
well-ordered societies
defined 41
and formal constraints on
conceptions of justice 89–91
and global justice 153–4
and problem of stability 136–40

CPSIA information can be obtained
at www.ICGtesting.com
Printed in the USA
LVHW04s2044220818
587778LV00013B/238/P